MUSIC FOR THE HANDICAPPED CHILD

MUSIC
FOR THE
HANDICAPPED
CHILD

JULIETTE ALVIN

Second Edition

LONDON
OXFORD UNIVERSITY PRESS

Oxford University Press, Walton Street, Oxford OX2 6DP

OXFORD LONDON GLASGOW
NEW YORK TORONTO MELBOURNE WELLINGTON
IBADAN NAIROBI DAR ES SALAAM LUSAKA CAPE TOWN
KUALA LUMPUR SINGAPORE JAKARTA HONG KONG TOKYO
DELHI BOMBAY CALCUTTA MADRAS KARACHI

ISBN O 19 314920 6

© *Oxford University Press, 1965*

Cover photograph reproduced
by kind permission of Dr. Otto Preu

First published 1965
Second edition 1976
Reprinted 1977 ●

Printed in Great Britain
at the University Press, Oxford
by Vivian Ridler
Printer to the University

To Jeanne Alvin

CONTENTS

Contents

INTRODUCTION

I BELIEVE that this book is the first of its kind to be written, and hope that it will open a door into a new and valuable field of research and study. It is designed not only for musicians and teachers but for anyone concerned with the development, the welfare, and the mental health of the handicapped child— parents, educationists, therapists, psychologists, and psychiatrists. They all try to develop the handicapped child to the limit of his potentials, to equip him for life, to help him to be stable and independent, and to find for him suitable creative activities which are the key to mental balance.

The special education and treatment of the handicapped child, which often starts in infancy, consists in team work between the family, the teacher, the physician, and the therapist. It cannot succeed unless all parties work together and are geared to a common goal, namely the welfare of a human being. The musician who wishes to make a significant contribution to the life of a handicapped child should learn enough about him to become an efficient member of the team. Each handicap presents specific problems of a physical, mental, or emotional nature to which music, as any other experience, has to be adapted.

A single book cannot exhaust a subject affecting the whole child, his needs, his personality, and his maturation, especially when the subject, namely music, is so extensive and has so many aspects and modes of application. I have tried to integrate my long and varied experience in playing or teaching music to children with my personal knowledge of work done by others in the same field. The methods described in this book rarely follow a conventional path; this would not be possible with handicapped children who do not usually fit in with normal procedures. For instance, the children I have worked with did not call me the music teacher. To the young ones I have been 'the Music Lady'; to all of them I have tried to be a friend, a musician who has shared with them the pleasure of making or listening to music, a music creative of joy, happiness, and harmony.

This book attempts to provoke a better assessment of the value of music to handicapped children. There is a vague agreement that 'music is good for them', or that 'they respond well to music'. But if this is so, could we not use music at a deeper and more effective level in order to help specifically towards the mental, emotional and social maturation of handicapped children in need of integrating and enriching experiences at their level? Could we not find out why music is good for them—why they respond so well to music—what are their responses due to, and what are their responses on which we could build? Furthermore, can we not find a relationship between their response to certain musical experiences and their mental, physical, or emotional state? And if so in which way could music contribute to their intellectual, social, or emotional development? We may also ask how musical experiences can be adapted to any kind or degree of handicap, so that the child can benefit from them.

So far, the answers to these questions have only skimmed the surface. This is not surprising since musicians, although devoted to the child, possess little if any knowledge of the nature and causes of the disability. They are not trained in the specialized teaching methods adapted to the child's handicap. Moreover, it is difficult for them to realize that music should contribute to the total development of the child and may be directed towards other ends than purely musical ones. On the other hand, specialists who fully understand and can assess the child's handicap rarely possess the musical skill or knowledge necessary to reach the child at a deep level. It is significant that there does not seem to exist a book on special education, however good, in which the chapter on music says anything substantial or revealing, in spite of the remarkable advance made recently in the treatment and education of the handicapped child. Musicians and specialists alike may be aware of the great unused potentials of music, but they are left without the special knowledge or guidance which they need.

Remedial music may help the mental, perceptual, or emotional growth of the handicapped child, irrespective of his musical aptitude or ability. Even the most severely handicapped child has normal basic needs for love, acceptance, security, and success, and he must also find means of self-expression at his own level. Music may be the only way he can realize himself. Music may represent to him a non-threatening world with which he can communicate, where he had known no failure, where he can integrate and identify himself. It may be a field in which he can use the restricted physical or mental means he possesses, however weak or deficient. Musical activities also can help him towards the awakening of perceptual awareness, the development of auditory discrimination and motor control.

But none of this can be achieved in a creative way unless constructive methods are devised. One cannot rely on trial and error or amateurism with the handicapped child who is so vulnerable and dependent.

The ideal which has guided me throughout the work is a conviction, based on fact, that music should be a creative experience, and that it should help to discover or exploit to the full any ability the child may possess in various fields, not necessarily in music. The handicapped child, unless quite exceptionally gifted, should not be expected to become a good performer of a normal standard, or to be able to understand complex music. There is a belief that a handicapped child is musically as good as a normal one, or even better. In fact, however, he will not achieve in music more than his general ability permits, a truth that applies to almost everything in his life, and has to be faced. If he seems to be more successful at music than at other subjects it is very much due to the extreme flexibility of music. Music can be adapted to make the best of any ability the child possesses, and to suit any mental, emotional or physical handicap. Even at the infant or pre-school stage, for instance, music can be an admirable means of non-verbal communication with the handicapped child.

In this book I discuss at length the correlation between the different stages of maturation of the handicapped child and his musical development. This correlation has been the key to my

approach. Since music affects mind, body, and emotions, I
have tried to grade the musical activities according to the
different aspects and stages of the child's development. With
a normal child this gradual process is usually straightforward
and follows an expected path. But with the handicapped child
the task is more complex. His emotional, mental, and physical
developments are not integrated, and the discrepancies or
conflicts of growth in his personality demand a skilful adaptation of the musical means. Moreover, every handicap creates
a ceiling of achievement above which the child will never reach.
We have to try to stretch him to the utmost, but we must never
lead him towards a wall against which he will stop and fail,
and give up. This need not happen with music.

The seeds of music can yield a rich harvest if their growth
responds to a need. Throughout the book indeed I discuss
music in terms of needs to be fulfilled. I believe that music has
something to offer to every handicapped child, not always in
strict musical terms, sometimes in an indirect way. The child's
individual response to music very often reveals a non-musical
need and shows how he can be reached and helped.

I also discuss the kind of musical experiences which can help
the child's social and emotional integration, and influence his
attitude towards play and work, towards himself and others.
Although in his own environment and at school the child is
protected, the team concerned with his welfare try to equip
him for adult life. The test of his education and treatment
occurs when he leaves school and has to face himself as an
individual belonging to a community. In this larger world he
may feel lost and lonely, and although he still has the same
needs for communication and self-expression, he has now out-
grown many of the child-like pursuits he used to enjoy. At that
crucial period of his life any means may help him which have
been gradually adapted and carried on from childhood and
adolescence to adulthood. I discuss this problem in relation
to musical activities and suggest how the transition can be
made so that the handicapped can have music and benefit
from it all his life. In this sense music can be called truly
creative.

THE STORY OF JOHN

John was one of the many children at the hospital. He had muscular dystrophy, a killing disease for which there is no cure and which leads to a general paralysis. But the illness does not necessarily impair the mind, and John continued to be a normal child with a desire to learn. He had to go into hospital, but there was a school at the hospital and he received schooling as well as medical treatment. Being a naturally easy, sociable, and courageous child, he accepted his condition and integrated quite well with the life in the ward.

Everyone knew that John, who had already lost the use of his legs, would be a permanent wheel-chair case, and get worse and worse. His hands were already showing signs of stiffness. Since treatment could only delay the effects of the disease it was important that the boy's schooling should give him all possible means of mental and emotional development and enable him to enjoy life as much as possible until the end.

Music was one of the most flourishing subjects taught at the hospital; there was music in every ward, singing, playing instruments, listening to music, musical theory and appreciation. Fortunately John was musically sensitive. The music teacher helped him to make his own bamboo pipe, a very exciting experience, and John kept it with his own small properties. He was taught to play well and seriously, learnt musical notation, and became an enthusiastic and knowledgeable listener to music as well as a proficient player and singer. In time John's musical equipment became the foundation of his life through which he expressed himself and had access to the wide and rich world of music. His pipe playing became so good that he was invited to join the music group of the staff. He helped to entertain visitors and took part in most of the hospital shows. He became a valuable member of the school ensemble even when his fingers became weaker and less flexible. He was helped by the fact that the bamboo pipe requires very little muscular strength and need not be held by the fingers. It can be leant on a table which supports the weight of the instrument. John could also sing quite well, and little by little he acquired a splendid repertoire of short tunes and songs. He could read music notation and was even able to follow on the score recorded performances of chamber or symphonic music. This increased his intelligent and sensitive appreciation of music.

Little by little, as he became older and more aware of his condition, John started to lose hope of recovery, and his love of and need for music increased. He had more difficulty in playing his pipe and in singing, but he passed much time listening actively to music with other children or by himself. Music also helped him to spiritualize his experiences and answered his need for beauty and harmony. Sometimes he also enjoyed the relaxing atmosphere brought by the presence of peaceful background music, on which time flows without conflict and is a help against a feeling of solitude.

John is not expected to live much longer, but his beloved music will follow him to the end. It is difficult to imagine what his short life would have been without music.

THE STORY OF GEORGE

George, a little boy of ten, was not happy, although nothing seemed to worry him particularly. He did not remember his father, who died when he was an infant, and he got on quite well with a half-brother born from his mother's second marriage.

George was intelligent, above the average, very nervous and unstable, unkempt and disorderly. Although he had done music and movement as a young child he was physically incredibly awkward.

He was having great trouble at school, always at the bottom of his form, and got increasingly bad reports which were a source of conflicts with his family. The boy was careless, inattentive, and seemed unable to pull himself together. He was going a bad way and seemed not to care.

At that time music came into his life. He had heard at home a recording of *Swan Lake* and was reached in an extraordinary way by the 'cello part in the score. He identified himself at once with the tune and asked if he could learn the 'cello. When I met him for the first time and asked him why he wished to learn the 'cello, he answered with eagerness that he wanted to be able to play 'that tune'. I knew nothing then about the child except that he had the right kind of motivation, that he looked very nervous and that he was probably in need of a means of self-expression.

I learnt so much from him about his life, even from the first lesson, that I tried to hide from him the fact that he was quite unfit to play a musical instrument. He had positively no ear, no rhythm, no motor control, and he always moved the wrong way. But he truly loved music and was set on 'playing that tune', although I had made it quite clear to him that he could not achieve it before a long time and without hard work.

I gathered very soon that he suffered from loneliness. From the first day he kept his instrument in his room and told me: 'My 'cello, that is my best pal. I put it in my room somewhere I can see it when I wake up.' We plodded along with meagre results, and I sometimes wondered about the wisdom of continuing when the musical results were so unsatisfactory, but he never lost his initial motivation. This child was looking for some kind of satisfactory relationship through which he could express himself. He felt he could find it in his 'cello. After a few weeks he told me that he had had a dream in his sleep: he was in an orchestra and played 'that tune'. The same dream occurred several times, and each time he was in a different orchestra.

There was then nothing else to do than to go on with much patience and understanding and to call on all the experience needed in such a laborious teaching task. Little by little he told me about the difficulties of his life. He had given up the idea that he could ever be good at school: there was a family crisis every time the school report arrived, and he was becoming quite callous about it. But he thought he would be good at playing the 'cello.

I made his 'cello become a means of rehabilitation. Each of the reports I sent at the end of term contained some of his good features such as eagerness, goodwill, punctuality, and so on, which gave a true and better picture of the boy. This helped to ease the family relationship and the boy was quite aware of it.

But the main rehabilitation to be done was in the boy himself. The lessons were an occasion to make him evaluate himself and face his shortcomings. He was careless, unable to criticize himself or to accept criticism, and had no standard in anything. His musical motivation was so strong that I could demand from him all he could give without making him feel that his best was mediocre. In fact, the demands made on him by a teacher he respected and admired made him feel that she respected him and had confidence in his ability to do better.

This relationship helped him to become stronger, more stable, to lose his indifference, and to regain his self-respect. At the same time the 'cello became to him a great source of emotional satisfaction and his love of music increased.

His nervousness and sense of inferiority had made contacts very difficult for him. The change from primary to secondary school might have proved to him a very difficult time. But he integrated at once with his new school because of his 'cello, through which he became a member of the orchestra. He felt he had something valuable to offer to his new school, and he started to form happy relationships through his music first, with the pupils and masters.

From that day he never looked back, and his personality developed normally. He had found himself through his love for a tune that had moved him and led him, with proper guidance, to know, to evaluate, and to express himself. He is now grown-up, but his 'cello is part of his life, and perhaps still 'his best pal'.

NOTE TO THE SECOND EDITION

In April 1971 a statutory change took place in Britain. The severely handicapped children who had been the responsibility of the Local Health Authorities were transferred to the Local Education Authorities. This fundamental change affected the Training Centres for children of school age, which became Special Schools. Therefore, when applied to Britain, the words 'Training Centre' should now read 'Special School' throughout this book.

1

THE MUSICAL SENSIBILITY OF
THE HANDICAPPED CHILD

MUSICAL sensibility is a disposition which provokes a pleasurable reaction to musical sounds, the pleasure being of a physical, a sensuous, an intellectual, or an emotional nature. It should not be confused with musical aptitude, which is the power to acquire some kind of creative or performing musical skill, and may stay dormant if the opportunity to develop it is lacking. The distinction between musical sensibility and musical aptitude is of particular importance in remedial education.

Handicapped children react to musical experiences exactly as normal children do. They are not more sensitive to music than others, but to them music can have special significance because it may be a substitute for impossible things, or a means of self-expression and communication better than others—even sometimes the only possible one.

Many handicapped children possess unsuspected musical aptitude, but this aptitude is usually impaired by the handicap. In remedial education we try to discover and to develop to their utmost any potentials which exist, even at a low degree, and musical aptitude may be one of them.

The following classification of children's musical sensibility and aptitude includes all types of children, normal or handicapped. (i) A child who possesses both musical sensibility and musical aptitude with the motivation to study has all the chances to develop high ability. (ii) A child who possesses musical aptitude and little sensibility may nevertheless become a good performer and derive great joy from it. (iii) A child who possesses neither is emotionally negative or indifferent to music. His social needs, however, may prompt him to join a group of children making music. I have never found a child who would not do so if means at his level could be found, and who did not enjoy, not the music itself, but the participation in a group activity. This activity may even awake in him some liking for, or interest in, music. (iv) The child who reacts adversely to music and does so for physiological or psychological reasons. For instance, certain sounds, the frequency or the intensity of the vibrations, may disturb his auditory apparatus—or on the other hand he may reject music for a deep-seated emotional reason. Whatever the case any adverse reaction to music of a handicapped child has causes that should be investigated, since it might lead to valuable information on some trouble perhaps yet not detected. (v) I have left to the end the child who is sensitive to music but possesses no aptitude. He is one of many and often fares very badly. His sensitivity to music may be un-discovered, for instance if he sings out of tune or cannot discriminate between different rhythmical patterns or sounds. This child may be branded as unmusical and exposed to a quite unjustified humiliation if, for instance, he is left out of the choir and given no substitute. Some teachers seem to assess the musical sensibility of a child only on his performing ability. Dr. Herbert Wing remarks that 'such opinions of school teachers are based chiefly on singing ability which may, or may not, be indicative of general musical capacity'.[1]

In the course of his research on musical talent Dr. Wing has also observed that a dislike for music was found in the musical as well as in the unmusical. This was sometimes due to emotional causes; for instance, one adolescent 'had been told as a young child that he had no musical aptitude; this not only caused him to dislike music but tended to make him think that it was useless to try to appreciate or understand music'.[2]

When a teacher has to deal with large groups of children it is scarcely possible for him to give individual attention to the child who is sensitive to music but shows no aptitude. The situation is different in special classes with small numbers and individual teaching. There every care should be taken to make this child participate in some musical activity and to give him a part in which his lack of ability will not disturb the group.

[1] *Tests of Musical Ability & Appreciation* (1948). For fuller details of this and later footnote references, see the Bibliography, p. 149.
[2] op. cit., p. 67.

This child should also be given frequent opportunities to listen to music and to develop his love for it. All musical experiences under proper guidance have value in the emotional maturation of any child, and especially of the handicapped, whose experiences are necessarily so limited.

THE ASSESSMENT OF MUSICAL SENSIBILITY

Psychologists and musicians agree that musical sensibility is based on an emotional response to music and that these emotional responses cannot be measured scientifically. The most complete work on the assessment of musical talent is by Carl Seashore, who has devised a number of standardized tests. But he himself states that 'musical reflections and emotions are examples of talents which are too diffuse to be measured although we can weigh many of the factors which are determining components'.[3] Aaron Copland is of the opinion that 'listening is a talent we possess in varying degree. . . . There is no reliable way of measuring the gift for listening.'[4]

In his experiments on musical tests Seashore has been able to measure the ability to receive auditory impressions from musical elements such as pitch, duration of sounds, and rhythmical patterns. He has tested the memory of sound and rhythm, the appreciation of timbre, and so on. He has made an illuminating study of the auditory perception of musical elements and of their possible relation to intellectual or mental ability. For instance, he states that no high intellectual process is involved in the perception of pitch or intensity, but when memory, logic, or judgement between auditory perceptions are involved, musical perception depends to some extent on the intelligence of the listener. Dr. Wing is of the same opinion and states that 'both musical ability and musical appreciation are qualities of the whole mind',[5] but his tests do not reveal any direct correlation between all-round musical capacity and education or intelligence.

These tests and many others on musical talent register and

[3] *Psychology of Musical Talent* (1919), p. 5.
[4] *Music and Imagination* (1952), p. 18.
[5] op. cit., p. 3.

measure accurately not the emotional response but the perceptual ability of the auditor, his memory of sound organized through pitch and duration. It is interesting to note that experienced musicians do not do particularly well in these tests. The reason may be that they are too conditioned to the interpretation of sounds, and cannot easily dissociate them from their emotional or intellectual meaning. It is obvious that a fine sense of hearing enhances the response to music but it does not in itself produce an emotion, just as we cannot assume that fine eyesight produces a love of art. We cannot draw a line between the physiological and the psychological effect of sound, although we can assert that a very high degree of musical sensitivity and achievement rests on a high ability to perceive as well as to interpret sounds. This high ability is at its optimum in musical prodigies and geniuses, in great composers and performers alike.

But this book is not concerned with high standards of achievement, perhaps not even with ordinary standards, since remedial music is used as a means and not as an end in itself. The musical achievement of a handicapped child is necessarily related to his condition and very often he may not be able to achieve much in any field. Nevertheless the musical results he achieves always reach deeper and wider than the standard of his musical performance would indicate.

If we wish to test the musical sensibility of a child for remedial purposes it is better done by observing his spontaneous reaction to any music which makes an impact on his mind and on his emotions. Though there is an infinite range of responses, they can be broadly classified, not precisely enough for standardized measurements but sufficient for a musical 'diagnosis'. This can be a guide towards a fair assessment of the child's musical sensibility without which no valuable use of remedial music is possible.

THE AUTHOR'S EXPERIMENTS

For a number of years I have made many experiments on the response to music of normal and handicapped children. My work is based on their reaction to the fundamental elements of music, namely speed, tone colour, pitch, volume, intensity, rhythm, and melody. These provoke in all children spontaneous and specific responses which reveal much more than their perceptual ability.

In my work with handicapped children I try to assess their need for emotional, intellectual, or realistic experiences. The music I play to them is related to their own experiences and can provoke in them a number of mental or emotional associations which are beneficial. This therapeutic approach is based on the power of music to affect the mood of the child, to stimulate his mind, and to release his emotions, as the case may be.

Handicapped and normal children alike show four major reactions to music: (*a*) the physical, (*b*) the sensuous, (*c*) the intellectual, (*d*) the emotional. This last is the crucial one with regard to musical sensibility.

(*a*) Almost all children react instinctively to the impact of rhythm which provokes primitive, dynamic physical reactions. (*b*) Many children are also sensitive to the sensuous effect of tone, a pleasurable sensory stimulation similar to the effect of certain colour on the eye, or certain materials on the touch. (*c*) Some children react intellectually. Their intelligence comes into action: they want to know, to understand, to remember, to discriminate. They may be interested in the structure of music; they have curiosity but may not be emotionally involved. (*d*) The child who is sensitive to the emotional impact of music finds in music an expression of feelings he has experienced and moods that he knows. To him music is part of his world. He may find in music love, security, movement which to him is life, excitement, aggressiveness, sadness, calm, joy, and many other feelings through which he can identify himself with the music. A number of children possess visual and auditory imagination which is stimulated by a musical experience and makes music alive and exciting. This reaction involves mind and emotion.

The responses to music of handicapped children show in the same way as with normal children, obviously within their physical or mental limitations. But even when they are inarticulate or crippled one can observe the light in their eyes, the expression on their face, their posture, the position of their hands, their silence or their speech, their tension or their relaxation, and many other signs of pleasure, dislike, excitement, or joy which can be noticed and interpreted by an experienced observer.

When a child shows a reaction of pleasure to music, whether a physical, a sensuous, an intellectual, or an emotional one, we can conclude that that child is sensitive to music in some way, and that music can be of value in his education. This is even truer of the handicapped, who more than any other needs enriching experiences that may be so few because of his condition. Whatever the condition of the child his emotional maturation depends on the nature and depth of his experiences and music may be one of them.

The limitations imposed by the handicap may show more severely when the child has a desire to sing or to play an instrument. Here we meet the question of musical aptitude, as distinct from musical sensibility.

Musical aptitude is based on a natural instinct for music which includes a number of factors, namely a good co-ordination between mind and body and the motor control necessary to acquire specific reflexes. A good singing voice, a trainable hand rest on muscular control. The possession of a trainable ear is also necessary, as well as the ability to understand the relation between sound and written symbols in order to learn musical notation.

Some children possess an innate facility, or a creative gift, and some even have a natural disposition to play a specific musical instrument, which it is important to discover from the start. But these precious endowments are no definite proof of innate musical sensibility, and a music teacher may discover an emotional deficiency towards music in a pupil who has shown promising musical aptitude.

Emotional factors play a vital role in the development and the crystallization of musical aptitude into musical ability. Emotional motivation, that is the child's desire or urge to express himself through music, is by far the most important. This urge may enable a child who has mediocre aptitude to do well enough, and it can work miracles with a physically or mentally handicapped child.

When we do music with these children we have to try un-orthodox methods and use an imaginative approach not to be found in textbooks. A great amount of musical knowledge and skill is necessary to make full use of the infinite means of adaptation that can be found in music. The class-room tech-niques through which adaptation to a specific handicap can be made are described in each relevant chapter. We are here concerned with general responses to music.

CHILDREN'S RESPONSES

During a number of years I have collected hundreds of free compositions written by children of all ages and of all types, essays which they have written after attending a concert. In these compositions the children expressed their impressions and feelings, stated their likes and dislikes in a candid and un-inhibited way. The children came from special schools or hospitals all over the country, from London, from small towns or villages, or from suburbia, and they represented a wide range of background, intelligence or ability, and all kinds and degrees of physical and emotional disabilities. They were suffering from subnormality, crippling diseases, cerebral palsy, or emotional disturbance.

Among the hundreds of essays in my possession there are only two which express complete indifference to music, and they were by normal children.

Dear Madam, I do not like music I don't know why, but if I liked it I would have enjoyed yours very much (*boy 7*).

I am not a musical type and that is that. The pieces played at the concert were simple enough for me to follow, but I found no pleasure in being able to do so. I have tried before to summon up some interest in music but I always finish even more convinced that I shall never like it (*boy 15*).

In the course of the work I have never met a handicapped child showing such complete indifference. Some of them reacted badly to music. A disturbed girl of nine stated that she did not like the piano part in The Elephant because it was too loud, and another one found the music too noisy. But even so I found that all the children I worked with could be touched by some element in the music. Each of the pieces performed contained one dominant element which they could perceive easily. Among those were speed, tone colour or timbre, pitch, volume, intensity, rhythm, and melody. I observed again and again that unsophisticated children were not easily struck or disturbed by harmonic dissonance and that since their response to it was noticeable only when the dissonance was emphasized by a rhythmical accentuation, the effect on them was clearly made by the rhythm more than by the dissonance itself. They were musically too immature to perceive, enjoy, or reject harmonic dissonances. On the other hand, some psychotic or deeply disturbed children seemed to react strongly to dissonant music in which there is much unresolved tension. Many children, once they were trained, enjoyed the kind of dissonance that adds colour and character to music, provided that the music had rhythmical stability. Nevertheless we found that children of a conformist type did not accept music which to them did not seem to conform to an accepted pattern.

Most children were sensitive to the sequence of intervals that forms a melodic pattern. They reacted well to the smoothness and continuity of a musical line, such as in 'The Swan', and to the effect of surprise and humour made by an unexpected interval between two notes, for instance what they called 'a big jump' made them laugh.

The element of speed provoked in them emotional reactions and created different moods, emotions, and sensations, not all of them pleasurable:

I liked the Elephant because it was clumsy and loud and kept me awake. For one that was slow and calm I nearly fell asleep. I did not like the Air because it was slow and made me feel tired (*backward boy 10*).

I liked it because it was fast and jolly and it was very nice when you played fast with your fingers (*backward girl 12*).

I liked the concert very much. I liked the Swan best. I like that one becurse it was nice and slow and carm and smooth (*backward boy 8*).

Some handicapped children found it difficult to follow fast music, and this was well expressed by a backward girl of ten who wrote, 'I liked the slow music better because you can hear it more plainly.'

The handicapped children with whom I worked became, like normal ones, well aware of pitch, speed, and intensity. But they were often confused about the meaning of words such as low and high, fast and slow, loud and soft, with regard to musical sounds. They used the words indiscriminately, although they seemed quite conscious of the impression they had received from a specific musical element. The following show much confusion in words:

This week we had a new tune about a Butterfly. It was just right, not too loud and not too soft [meaning fast and slow] (*disturbed E.S.N. boy 9*).

When you touched a string at the bottom it was loud, and when you touched a not at the top it was soft [meaning high and low] (*disturbed E.S.N. girl 10*).

I found that psychotic and cerebral palsied children and all children suffering from nervous tension reacted strongly to certain sequences of sounds. The pentatonic scale had a definitely sedative effect. I often noticed too that low frequency sounds made a soothing effect, and that tense children relaxed when they heard a piece played in the low register, even if the piece was exciting in itself.

Effects of increasing or decreasing volume or intensity provoked in the children the same reactions as high or low frequency, namely an exciting or calming effect. In consequence they used indiscriminately the words high for loud and slow for soft.

Rhythmical or dance music of a simple kind provoked a general physical reaction, an urge to move and to dance. The following remark from a thirteen-year-old E.S.N. girl is typical: 'The Highland Dance made you filled like dancing to it. I would like to hear it all over again.' Or the remark of a spastic boy that 'you can follow the music better by tapping your fingers'.

But if rhythm gives pleasant feelings to most children, the physical reaction it provokes may be disturbing to those in need of relaxation. Music in which there is a repetitive and percussive element can make on them the same adverse effect as high frequency or intensity often do. The feeling of liveliness and fast movement expressed in certain kinds of stimulative music may become to nervous children an agent of compulsive excitement and be harmful. In consequence when the children were tense and disturbed I tried not to provoke responses that would have been undesirable.

It would be a mistake to judge the musical sensibility of young children on their reaction to rhythm alone. Musically sensitive children respond readily to melody, that is to a succession of consonant and relatively slow notes which gives a pleasurable feeling of continuity without disturbing contrasts of pitch or rhythm. Children often used the word 'smooth' or 'sweet' in this respect, and the words seemed to express sensuous pleasure as well. They commented also on the mood of the melody and on any image attached to a particular piece. Some of the children expressed feelings of a deeper nature and a real appreciation of beauty. The young child who said that he liked slow music better because it was more loving was a truly sensitive child, and so was the thirteen-year-old crippled boy who wrote: 'The piece I liked best was the Air by Bach witch was quiet and peaceful.'

Throughout the experiments we observed the usual types of reaction to music, namely the imaginative, the realistic, the intellectual, or the purely emotional through identification. Many children were quite aware of the happiness music brought them.

The emotionally mature children were naturally more conscious than the immature ones of the impact music made on them. Although most of them were not able to express it as well as normal children do, music seemed to answer some of their unspoken and unfulfilled needs. .

The feeling that music was realistic and humorous appealed to them all. 'What I liked best', wrote a big backward fourteen-year-old boy, 'was the Swan, I like the rippling of the piano . . . the cat and the mouse was very good, you could seem to imagine wailing outside the hole for the mouse it was funny. . . .' Another backward fifteen-year-old boy expressed his opinion in a child-like fashion:

I thoght you picket the right songs not too operatic. And the song I like in the animals was the cat and the MACE and it was a change becouse it made you laugh.

We found that the children who experienced more pleasure when they were aware of the precise meaning of the music usually lacked the imagination that accompanies sensitivity. A piece with a story was not necessary to arouse the emotions of the musically sensitive children. But from time to time it helped to renew and sustain the attention of children whose musical and all-round imagination was poor.

We observed that the auditory and visual imagination of the more gifted children was much stimulated by the music—a reaction that was emotionally and intellectually creative. A number of their essays contained delightful pictures called to their mind by the music and some were truly poetical. Many were related to the child's own emotional or perceptual experience.

Evocative and colourful music without a story but introduced with an imaginative title was successful with most children, for instance pieces like The Swan, Lullabies, Granadina, Nonsense piece, Habanera, The Elephant, and so on. Those provoked the imagination of even retarded children. 'The music makes me think of the Swan swimming in the water,' wrote an E.S.N. boy of nine. And a fourteen-year-old E.S.N. girl wrote in her book: 'The Swans are swaiming down the stream with her little bubychicks. The ripples are round them. . . .' And further on: 'The to buby are called Keith and Andy they are both boy and they are going to sleep with the Cradle song.'

The following lines were written by a cripple boy of fourteen in an orthopaedic hospital, and it is characteristic to read how much he was touched by an experience of movement. Moreover, he illustrated his essay with a lively picture of dancers:

SPANISH DANCERS

The Spanish dancers dance very quickly and stamp their feet loudly on the floor. They wear hard shoes and have castanettes in both hands. They swirl and twist about and click their castanettes with great speed.

As we listened to the Cello play, in our mind's eye we saw the Spanish dancers and all the colour and gaiety of Spain.

The Elephant appeals particularly to E.S.N. children who often refer to the piece. Here is a complete, unusually good composition by a fourteen-year-old E.S.N. girl:

THE ELEPHAINT

Once upon time there was a Elephant, He was fat, He had a big trunc and a little tail and Had two big ears. His legs were fat too. He was learning haw to dance but could not and sat down and cried. The he got up and found that he cauld dance and went home happy and lived happily ever after.

Beauty in music is the result of many components we may not be able to analyse and to which some children react deeply. In spite of some poverty in their vocabulary, the words 'beautiful' or 'wonderful' sometimes appear in these essays, as opposed to 'pretty' or 'nice' which usually reflect a more superficial feeling, or simply a physical reaction to stimulative music. The E.S.N. girl of fourteen who liked the Swan because 'it is beautiful and sad'—and the paralysed boy of thirteen who wrote: 'The Air on the G string was wonderful and gave a feeling of peace and solitude' had been deeply moved by the sheer beauty of the music.

When children have an experience in which their intelligence is involved they use the words 'interesting' or 'thinking' which expresses a more mature mind. These words rarely occur in the essays of very young children. Some older children react not to the music itself but to some other sides of the performance, reaction which does not indicate musical sensibility but interest in, for instance, the instrumental technique. This reaction may prove useful to the discovery of some potential performing aptitude. The children who respond both intellectually and emotionally are the better equipped and may achieve a great deal in music. The purely intellectual, non-emotional reaction to music is not musically promising, but it can help us to discover in the child some interest that may be developed even in other fields than music. The following essays amount to a good description of an experience; they show a good sense of observation and a fair memory for facts. These are the words of a fourteen-year-old backward boy:

When I first heard you were coming I did not think that it would be any good listening to your music until you started talking about it, I watched you move your fingers up and down the strings to make a TOTALY new note and I watched you move your bow made out of horse-hair up and down keeping it on the strings for a long note, and just a inch of bow to make a short sharp note. . . .

This description, from a fifteen-year-old E.S.N. girl, is worth quoting in full:

THE CELLO IS MADE

The bow is made out of a house tails. The top were the keys thats made out of black Eemony the back part is made of pine wood, that shop in the picture that were they sold it they are called string instruments they youse propler for the front part of the Cello. the keys halp to tighten the strings the yose roson for the bow they rub some white stuff up and down on the bow so that is well stick so it will not keep the Reson is made out of scots pine wood. they holed in the tree and out comes some stuff and that makes the reson the strings are made out of lames gut the top of the bow is made out of palm the leg is made out of popele tree.

During a performance many children identified themselves with the music, or with the performer, or with the instruments, a frequent and conspicuous process with handicapped children. Music which is movement through time enables them to go through an experience in which fantasy and reality are combined.

In the following two essays an E.S.N. boy age eleven and an E.S.N. girl age twelve heard the same story in music, of 'The Cat and the Mice'. Both essays are written in the first person, the boy identified with the cat, and the girl with the mouse, but she gave the mouse a masculine name.

My name is Fiddler, and I am a very proud cat. I thought of a good Idea so that I could get the mice out of their holes. I will sing to them and then they will come out. I said 'come out dear mice, and play with me' and I sang to them very sweetly. So the mice came out of their holes. But then I sprang on the silly mice and gobbled them up. Only one of the mice went back in his hole alive.

The girl's essay had a title:

THE CAT AND THE MICE

I am a careful mouse. My name is Tommy. When I was playing happily under the floor I just heard the cat singing a beautiful song. This is the song he was singing: 'Come out to play with me, dear mice.' So all my friends came out one by one. The cat sprang and gobbled them up, all except me—lucky me!

During the performance many children watched and imitated the movements of the 'cellist or the pianist. A number of them built up a close and silent relationship with the musicians. The form in which they wrote their essays disclosed their level of emotional maturity. The immature children wrote a personal letter, the others wrote more impersonally. A backward teenager expressed himself in the following direct way: 'I like the cello very much, if I could play like you I'd certainly think I was a marvel.' Or: 'I like the sound of the cello you played it as if your heart was devoted to it and you could see you liked it as much as I liked it.'

The music book of an E.S.N. girl of fourteen contained the following essay:

THE CELLO CONCERT

I enjoyed listening to you.
I expect the others liked it very much.
I like the way you play the cello.
I like the Elephant best of all and the cat and the mouse.
The cello can skip, hop, run, dance, march.
I like the lillaby too and the shepherd song and you
played it very nice and you are very clever indeed.

Handicapped children whose intelligence was not maimed often wrote in the most expressive and imaginative way. I should like to quote essays written by two adolescent boys in hospital in an orthopaedic ward.

THE TREE

Trees of all kinds are graceful and beautiful. They clothe our country-side with a cloak of green, and bring untold joy into our hearts.

When a tree is felled and its beauty lives no more, sometimes that beauty lives again in another form. The wood is fashioned into objects of good design and brings us pleasure. The cello is made from a noble tree, and brings to us all the natural beauty of the tree in a different way. It sings a song of all that is lovely in this world.

SHEPHERD AND HILLSIDE

Music paints a picture.

On the hillside far away a lonely shepherd was with sheep. We could see this picture as the cello played softly with the mute fixed on the bridge. It was as if it came from the silent hills of SCOTLAND.

Many of these essays showed in the child a single or at least a dominant response to music, whether of an emotional, a physical, or an intellectual kind. But a number of children were reached in every way and each of their essays contained all the essential responses to music. The following one came from a backward girl of eleven:

THE CONCERT

I liked the Concert very much. I liked the sonata, the Swan and the little Donkey. They were my best music. It must be hard to play with a bow. Cello is a funny word to spell. They made such a lovely [tune] the notes. It was very pleasant music like a lulaby It [was] so sweet and joyful. It would be nice to dance to it. I liked it very much.

The boy of sixteen who wrote the next essay was paralysed, and to him the first musical performance was a revelation. He reacted to all aspects of music, to its emotional, aesthetic, and sensuous appeal, to its imaginative and descriptive power, and to the attraction of the instrument:

THE CELLO RECITAL

I thought that an hour listening to a cello would be a boring prospect. But now, after the performance I am realy glad that I went. I am amazed at the way the cellist could adapt the instrument to make so many different sounds. The Air on the G string was wonderful and gave a feeling of peace and solitude. As a contrast the next piece was happy and joyful.

I will not go into detail on all the pieces but it was interesting to see how she made all the different aspects. The mute gave a feeling of distance and was used very expertly in the tune about the shepherds. The tunes about the Elephant, Butterfly and Swan really showed what can be done with a cello. The Swan's smooth and graceful movements were clearly shown, while the big sounds of the heavy Elephant was the exact opposite. The Butterfly was so light that one could really imagine the little creature flitting about among the flowers.

I hope to hear something similar at the earliest possible moment.

CONCLUSION

This specific experimental work with handicapped children was done without a preconceived programme. I tried to find means of developing their perception of sound and their interpretation of music. I started at their own level of mental and emotional maturity, observed their responses, and took my direction from them. At the same time I guided and followed them at their own pace of development.

Their responses were of many different kinds, the kinds music provokes in any audience. The quality and depth of the children's responses showed a marked increase as their auditory perception and their span of attention developed. The joy and happiness they displayed in the process were a sign that the experience answered a need. Most of the children were ready to make the effort I asked from them, through direct or indirect means. It was satisfactory to note that in the course of the long and extensive work I found no handicapped child who, within his own limitations, did not gain something from the experience or did not display some kind of musical sensibility.

2

MUSIC AND THE MATURATION
OF THE HANDICAPPED CHILD

GENERAL MATURATION

Music can contribute to the general growth of the handicapped child in many ways. For instance, as a substitute for other activities; as a compensation since it can bring reward and achievement; as an agent of sensory development; as an emotional outlet; as a mental stimulus; as a means of socialization. These many aspects of a single factor give music an integrating power because they are indissolubly linked with one another and they involve the mind, body, and emotion of the child in one experience.

The maturation of the handicapped child is often delayed or unevenly distributed on account of his sensory, emotional, or mental disability which prevents a general co-ordinated development. Physical, intellectual, emotional, and social developments are so closely interwoven that a handicap affecting only a specific area of the child's development is bound to hamper his harmonious growth. It is thought that the most valuable means of maturation are those which can integrate the different parts of the child's development and appeal to his whole being. This applies particularly well to music, since it can offer the handicapped child a vast number of sensory, emotional, intellectual, and social experiences, some of which he may not be able to get by any other means. Moreover, it is flexible enough to be adapted not only to the specific disability of the child but also to each of the stages of his maturation.

This and the next chapters discuss the value of musical experiences in relation to the emotional, intellectual, and social development of the handicapped child. This approach is somewhat arbitrary since it is difficult to dissociate these different elements, but it may help to clarify the argument.

EMOTIONAL MATURATION

The child's emotional maturation depends on the variety and the richness of his emotional experiences. During babyhood, childhood, and adolescence he gradually develops affective relationships and passes from the egocentric stage to the understanding of more mature emotions. For the handicapped child perhaps even more than for the normal child music can reflect and assist this emotional maturation because it is closely related to his emotional life—an emotional life which is often very complex. Since maturation is characterized by a growing awareness of self, the process may be distressing to the handicapped child who realizes increasingly the amount and the consequences of his disability in thé present and in the future. It is essential for him to find support in some emotional outlet of a creative nature such as music, through which he can express himself.

Emotional experiences can upset the mental balance of a child if they happen at a time he is not equipped to deal with them. A handicapped child is likely to suffer from great stress or tension not only because he cannot integrate or communicate normally, but because he frequently has to meet with situations he may not be able to deal with. He has to accept a disability without understanding why he is different from other children and deprived of what they normally enjoy as their birthright. There may never be an explanation of why a particular child has been afflicted. He may react to his affliction in various ways, become withdrawn and depressed; he may lose heart and give up the fight; he may stay dependent, demanding, and egocentric; he may become aggressive, destructive, or anti-social and reject contacts of all kinds. Whatever his reaction, he must be helped to keep or to regain his mental balance without which he cannot develop. He must be offered satisfying emotional experiences through creative activities of the kind suitable to his handicap and to his stage of maturity. He should also be helped to develop some means of self-expression at his own level.

Music can give this child numerous ways of integration and also adapt itself to his stage of development. Creative activities are an emotional outlet of the greatest value which integrate the child's emotional, physical, and mental experiences. Singing or playing an instrument even at a low level of achievement enable the child to utilize and to connect various perceptual and emotional experiences. Singing links together verbal and musical sounds and requires control of the singing and the speaking apparatus, a process which may become more and more conscious as the child develops. The manipulation of a musical instrument requires tactile sense and motor control as well as the use of auditory perception. The emotional desire to express himself in music may help and even hasten the perceptual maturation of the child.

Activities such as singing or playing an instrument are directly creative, since the child produces his own world of sounds.

Listening to music is another kind of musical experience, not a directly creative process, but a re-creative process in which the child interprets the sounds he hears and makes them his own in terms of his individual emotional experiences.

The growth of personality depends on the fulfilment of basic emotional needs which are the same in normal and handicapped children. Each of them needs to feel secure, loved, and accepted, to belong and to express himself. Only then can he relate and develop. The child finds security in the emotional stability and predictability of his environment which enable him to grow without fears or conflicts. But the handicapped child, even if he is loved and well cared for, is bound to experience fears and tension. He may feel deprived or frustrated and often lacks the necessary confidence to deal with new or unknown situations. Familiar experiences that can give him a feeling of security and protection can help him tremendously in times of anxiety or stress. I have seen in hospitals some children whose fears, anxiety, or feeling of solitude were greatly relieved by musical activities, which created a bridge between the familiar and the unknown world. Some hospitals for children use music to alleviate fears or boredom; in some of them the children are taught to make and to play their own bamboo pipe. They keep it in a little case under their pillow, and the small instrument gives them the feeling of a familiar presence, something to which they can relate, and a means of self-expression. The young patients, even the babies, are also encouraged to sing, and this music transforms the atmosphere of the wards. They seem to lose their frightening aspect.

The sense of security that the child needs can develop through association and familiarity with certain pleasurable experiences. This can apply to music: a baby who has been sung to by his mother may associate singing with a feeling of well-being and affection. We can expect that at an early stage of his development this child will sing spontaneously and then experience emotional satisfaction. It is beneficial to his musical development that he should first go through the purely intuitive irrational stage, in the exploration of sound, singing unconsciously or trying the notes of a keyboard or any other musical instrument—experiences through which he will become aware of his own familiar world of sounds. Later on when he is ready for association and co-operative activities his early experiences can help him to join other children in a music group. We can observe the value of musical activities as a means of emotional integration when he goes to school for the first time. This is to many handicapped children a traumatic experience. They may be leaving for the first time the familiar and protective environment of the home to go into an unknown world which may look threatening. A great number of special teachers use music to create immediate relationship with the child who may be frightened, shy, or unco-operative. Music-making among other activities may help to allay his fears and prevent him at once from developing an a-social attitude, or from withdrawing into babyish ways. When a handicapped child is emotionally immature he should be helped to grow out of his infantile behaviour and offered emotional experiences through which he can realize himself, but at the same time feel protected and secure.

Music-making, individually or in a group, can help towards the maturation of older handicapped children. It is an emotionally satisfying experience, to some of them an already familiar one, to others a new contact which may bring deep joy. In this new situation infantile attitudes are no more acceptable. The co-operation involved in a singing group, the handling of an instrument which must be used in a certain way and cared for, entail responsibility, and demand from the child a certain degree of emotional maturity.

PLAY AND WORK

At an early stage the child passes slowly from the conception of play to the conception of work. We can observe this development in music as well as in other fields. The child starts organizing his perceptual experiences and discriminating between familiar sensations. Even if this process is impaired or delayed by a handicap, irrational behaviour gives way to some concept of logic and order. Then we can observe the development of the conscious behaviour of the child, and the mental and physical effort he makes towards a desirable end. This development is quite noticeable when a child who is given a chance to handle freely sound-producing objects passes from the stage of irrational and indiscriminate manipulation of some musical instrument to the consciousness that certain sounds are agreeable and that it is desirable to find them and to repeat them. This process is obvious when a toddler explores by himself the keyboard of a piano, and tries one key after another unaided. A young baby under a year old not yet able to sing may well show a marked preference for a musical toy put at his disposal and that he can choose and handle himself. The 'play' stage in music is very valuable to the maturation of the child when it corresponds to the very early stage of his development. It is the first stage of the sensory exploration of musical sounds leading to their discrimination, the result of which is not yet 'music' since it is not organized sound. The child makes music only when he is ready to recognize and organize sound and to perceive some relationship of pitch or time, whether he sings or plays.

This first stage of 'play' passes more or less rapidly according to the emotional and mental stage of the child, who should be watched carefully and helped to enter the second stage as soon as he is ready for it. I have often observed that handicapped children are kept too long on immature musical activities which are supposed to bring them more enjoyment because they are not organized and entail no effort. The music teacher may not be aware that he is delaying a normal process of musical maturation. Purposeless or uncontrolled enjoyment rapidly becomes tedious and often frustrating to a child, and this is particularly true of music. Like all pursuits music at a certain stage of development involves an effort towards a desirable end for which some control is required. This control is best when it is self-imposed for the sake of the goal. The handicapped child may encounter physical difficulties in playing or singing, nevertheless the effort he makes towards a desirable musical end depends more on emotional motivation than on his ability. But the immature or the handicapped child is not always able to sustain any effort and has to become more mature before he can extend its duration.

Time, like work, is a creative concept which the young child does not understand. He has no ability to project himself in the future and is not much aware of the past. Only the present exists for him, he cannot wait for the fulfilment of a need or a wish, not because he is impatient, but because he is immature. This is the case with many handicapped children whose mind and emotions are rooted in the present, and it creates a number of educational problems. In music we should first offer him immediate gratification and help him to work gradually towards a more mature attitude. Little by little the musical results should be projected into the future. The musical achievement of the child may then take on a new dimension and become a new experience. Musical activities can easily be adapted to give the child the emotional satisfaction he needs at the right time, and can also help to develop and stretch his concept of time in terms of musical results.

The emotional motivation which can help to project an effort into the future is very striking in the autumn term when schools, including special schools, are preparing a Christmas musical programme. Even small children are caught in the spirit of projection towards Christmas.

A well-graded musical programme can help the child to work towards a specific achievement. From the beginning the smallest musical improvement can be detected by the child himself and he can enjoy it because the result is appreciable at once and he gets praise for it. During a short lesson he can learn the new verse of a song, improve his drumming technique, play one more note on his recorder or on his dulcimer, and those are concrete achievements, not easy to get so rapidly in other fields.

The musical transition from playing 'with' a musical instrument or using one's voice as it comes, to playing 'on' an instrument or singing rationally corresponds to the development of the concept of work, as against play. In the process the infantile need for immediate gratification can be replaced by a purposeful effort towards a future result. The music teacher should direct the process and grade it at the right time, otherwise the child may adopt towards musical activities a lazy attitude which will prevent any real progress and ultimately frustrate him. He will go on considering music as 'play' in an emotionally infantile way, he will dismiss or refuse to make the mental effort that brings reward. In consequence he will miss much of the benefit he could gain from musical activities. A normal child can afford to miss some of his opportunities, but a handicapped child must take all possible chances of development and achievement, however small, in any field open to him.

Although musical development and achievement require from the child a certain effort it is absolutely essential that one should never spoil the feeling of spontaneous joy and satisfaction that music can give. Uncontrolled emotional outlets are still acceptable in the early stages of maturation and may be beneficial to the disturbed immature child in need of emotional release. But even so they represent only a stage in the emotional and musical development of the child and should ultimately lead to a deeper and more complete relationship between the handicapped child and music, a relationship in which mind, emotion and body are integrated.

An increasingly mature attitude towards music in which

the mind is involved even in a small degree does not make music less enjoyable and satisfactory. On the contrary, it then develops into a deeper means of self-expression and identification.

IDENTIFICATION

Identification is an emotional process through which the child relates and belongs to his environment, a process which greatly helps in the development of his personality. The normal child finds around him numerous ways of identifying himself. The handicapped child, however, is deprived of many of the normal sensory or mental or emotional means of communication and cannot easily fit into the usual pattern of life. He is therefore likely to be a lonely and isolated being. Any means of identification through which he can relate to the world around him and mature is specially valuable to him.

Music can offer a sensitive child, especially the handicapped, such a means of identification through experiences which appeal to his emotions, to his imagination, and to his sense of realism, whether he listens to or makes music or sings. Children making or listening to music often display revealing signs of identification with the experience, through their facial expression, their posture, their rapt attention, their oblivion to the surroundings. This response is specially striking with handicapped children.

The sensitive child identifies with music which expresses feelings, moods, or sensations with which he is familiar. Therefore his kind of response to music depends on his emotional maturity. The feelings through which the child identifies with the music range from infantile sensations of calm or movement to mature, deep, and complex emotions. The same piece can evoke in children different kinds of reaction, depending on their individual emotional experiences through which they identify with the music. For instance, a simple traditional melody may give a very young child a familiar sensation of softness and smoothness, and to a more mature one a feeling of peace and serenity. Emotionally mature children can identify with music expressing such emotions as conflict, love, aggression, or anger. Violent feelings expressed in music can have a cathartic effect on a disturbed child which may be desirable if it is done under proper conditions. When the impact of the music brings to the surface deeply repressed emotions the child may be for a time overwhelmed and should be closely watched until he is liberated. This will be further discussed in the chapter on maladjustment.

Children themselves are often quite aware of the need they have for certain kinds of musical experiences. Neurotic and disturbed children sometimes ask me to play 'sad music', while emotionally healthy children ask for gay and lively pieces. Mentally alert children want to hear new pieces, the subnormal or the withdrawn choose again and again the same pieces which make them feel mentally and emotionally secure.

I have often observed and made use of the fact that the animistic character of music appeals to children whose world is still irrational. Music which moves in space and time, even when it is not descriptive or imitative, corresponds in some way to the animistic world of the child. For instance, many children learning musical notation would add legs or expressive faces to figures of minims or crochets, and subnormal adolescents are quite likely to do so. They say that the notes dance, run, or skip. Musical instruments too become personified and alive. The 'cello I use is Mr. Cello who speaks to them, behaves in certain pleasant or 'naughty' ways and goes to sleep in 'his' case.

Music provokes in a sensitive child not only feelings but many mental images through which he identifies with the experience, even more so if it is an experience of which he is deprived. For instance, when playing a Spanish piece I have seen crippled children imagine themselves dressed in Spanish costumes and enjoying the feeling of the dance, although they were not moving. During musical descriptions of animals such as the Elephant or the Butterfly one can observe many children, including the inarticulate or the withdrawn, acting as though they were elephants or butterflies. They also identify with people pictured in the music, such as the shepherd boy, the dancing doll, the old beggar, who live and move in the piece. This process of identification may be very valuable with emotionally disturbed children.

When the music is likely to evoke mental images and associations the accompanying verbal text should be kept to a minimum. A short title should suffice, leaving as much freedom as possible to the child's imagination and emotional response, except perhaps in the case of the retarded child who needs the help of combined stimulation. Otherwise words are too precise and may fetter the imaginative identification of the child who feels in terms of his own experience and not in verbal terms. The teacher who believes that children always prefer music with a story may be lacking in imagination.

ACHIEVEMENT

A sense of achievement and of progress is necessary to the emotional development of the handicapped child who so often meets with failure and discouragement. Achievement in any field can give this child self-confidence and assist the development of his character. It can also lead to an improved attitude towards work and increase of perseverance or greater readiness to accept criticism or temporary failure. The handicapped child needs much understanding to develop his personality. He needs the self-confidence and the feeling of being accepted that an immediate success can give, and the kind of encouragement which is an expression of other people's faith in his ability to overcome the obstacles facing him. This confidence based on an initial success can help the handicapped child to gain self-respect and optimism.

These feelings can grow out of well-planned musical activities largely because music always carries in itself an element o play and enjoyment. Therefore the child who sings or plays can derive great satisfaction from the activity itself and need not compete against others unless it would be helpful to him, since music is not essentially a competitive activity. The teacher may be as permissive or strict as the child's emotional state requires, irrespective of the standard of performance.

The child can achieve a great deal of self-knowledge through his own appraisal of his musical achievement. Musical activities can help him to develop a healthy attitude towards success or failure even from learning to play a little bamboo pipe. This self-appraisal can lead to more mature attitudes in situations involving other people such as his teacher or his fellows in a music group.

Much music-making is based on the imitation of some musical performance which sets a standard and provokes a motivation to act, a motivation which may be highly emotional. One should watch carefully the occasions likely to influence the desires of a handicapped child and stir up in him only those ambitions which can be realized at least in part and thus lead to an acceptable achievement—never to an ultimate failure.

The parents' illusions or the teacher's misguided good intentions sometimes influence the child, especially if he shows more aptitude for music than for other subjects—a frequent occurrence with subnormal children who are led to believe that they could learn a complex instrument such as the violin or the piano. In most cases this has unfortunate consequences if ultimately the child is bound to fail and to feel frustrated. He should be offered only a suitable musical instrument on which he can succeed—or some other form of creative activity.

ADOLESCENCE

During the difficult period of adolescence the musical and emotional development of a child are correlated in the same way as in childhood. This period is often distressing to the handicapped who undergoes the normal physiological and emotional changes and at the same time becomes more and more aware of the difference between him and the others. He is in danger of losing his mental balance which depends on the fulfilment of the need he has to feel secure and accepted and to find means of self-expression. He may reject what he has accepted hitherto because it no longer satisfies him. We should also expect a change in his attitude towards music. He may reject as childish the musical activities he has previously enjoyed and try new ways of making music. The adolescent may turn to pop music for the same reasons that he accepted music as a child: he finds in it an emotional outlet and a means to belong to a group. In rarer cases, he may seek in great music emotions of a deeper, more spiritual and aesthetic character.

The type of pop music that appeals to adolescents is so repetitive that it may well give them a feeling of security and protection. Their need for incessant music in the background and their ceaseless use of portable transistors indicate how insecure they feel unless there is a presence in the background to which they can relate either individually or as a group.

Moreover, all adolescents need hero-worship. From the traditional realm of physical prowess this worship has switched to the world of popular music. The hero is now the pop singer, male or female, who is good-looking, successful, famous, always in love, almost untrained, and who makes an incredible amount of money. He even provides his parents with comforts from his fabulous earnings, thus reversing the relationship of child to parent. He is simple in his habits and unspoilt in character. The insecure adolescent boy or girl, normal or handicapped, identifies easily with the pop singer, collects his pictures, spends much money on buying records of his songs and worships him as an individual who is what he would like to be. The pop songs usually have an infantile text and they mostly express immature feelings that the adolescent is ready to absorb and confuse with grown-up experiences.

Rock and Roll, Twist, and other dances associated with the musical world of the adolescent are an expression of the physiological sexual urge that a boy or a girl discovers in himself or herself. We may be perturbed if we only think of music and dancing as a cultural and aesthetic experience through the harmonious use of the body. Indeed music and dances are more than that. They can relate to our most primitive instincts in a crude form, to sex or violence, and can be a thoroughly non-intellectual experience which answers subconscious needs.

There may be less danger in accepting for the normal or handicapped child the music which appeals to him in his adolescence than in rejecting it or disapproving on aesthetic

or cultural grounds. If civilized music has really been integrated in the child's emotional maturation this need for pop
music and twist may last only during his disturbed adolescence.
Indeed, some children, especially the home-bound handicapped
ones, during that period are quite musically ambivalent. They
enjoy listening to concerts of classical music as well as to
performances of pop music.

But the non-classical music that appeals to the adolescent is
not all of the immature type. The appreciation of·real jazz,
whether hot or cold, requires a high standard of knowledge
and discrimination. It can offer the handicapped adolescent
a true emotional outlet of a more mature kind. This music
expresses at a higher mental and artistic level much of his
conflicting feelings. It may form a link between him and the
modern world of the normal adolescent.

At another level an adolescent may be looking for experiences that will appeal to his new emotions and sublimate them.
I have met many such cases among handicapped boys and
girls. In adolescence, says Dame Olive Wheeler, there is also
'an intensification and a refinement of the aesthetic emotions'.[1]
She holds that the education of the adolescent should include
'both the appreciation of beauty in various forms and its
expression in some chosen medium'. In music or some other
kind of creative activity, he should find help throughout a
difficult period of his life.

CONCLUSION

To sum up: the emotional maturation of the individual to
adulthood depends on his emotional experiences and on the
way he uses them. Music is an emotional experience that the
handicapped child can use in the process of his development.
Above all music can enable him to express himself; develop
his personality by creating healthy attitudes towards himself
and others; and evoke identification at his own emotional
level.

The contribution that music can make towards the emotional maturation of a handicapped child depends on the skill

[1] *Mental Health and Education* (1961), p. 107.

and knowledge of the musician in charge of the work, and on his understanding of the child's psychology and disability. Perhaps we need more musicians specially trained for this work if music is to play its full part in the emotional development of the handicapped child.

3

INTELLECTUAL MATURATION

THE growth of our consciousness and intelligence depends on the perceptual development that takes place in many fields. Music can be one of them, and although it rests on auditory experiences it may also help towards the development of visual and tactile perception and towards motor control.

Music is made of organized sounds and, as such, is a product of the human mind which gives order and shape to auditory perceptions. This mental organization of sound is among man's greatest accomplishments. It culminates in language, where sounds become symbolic through an accepted meaning and which require a high intellectual process to be interpreted and understood.

Music may be compared to language, but as it is non-verbal and non-symbolic it can, in its elementary forms, operate at low-brain level. Even so, its apprehension requires some kind of intelligence. From that lowest level, the apprehension of music can go up a scale of increasingly complicated mental operations to the understanding of the most complex combination of sounds. The human mind can be trained to perform amazing musical feats such as the silent reading of a full symphonic score or the perception of a minor error in a minor part during a full orchestral performance. This achievement requires a high degree of specific intelligence and discriminating auditory perception, and naturally does not apply to the handicapped child. However, on some degree of the vast scale of musical pursuits we can find activities suitable to every handicapped child, activities which stretch the mental faculty he possesses. We must know about the child's ability before deciding at which level we can begin. We cannot teach any child anything unless we begin where he is, at his own mental, perceptual, and emotional level. This approach has to be an individual one, since a handicapped child rarely fits into a general pattern.

DEVELOPING AUDITORY PERCEPTION

First, music should be considered in relation to the child's auditory perception and to the two processes of hearing and listening, which are quite distinct from one another.

We are much concerned in developing the visual perception of infants and children, who are incessantly told 'to look' or 'to see'—but they are much less often told 'to hear' or 'to listen' except with regard to speech. The result is that the child's auditory perception is imperfectly developed and he is not sufficiently aware of his auditory apparatus. The little savage may know more about the sounds of the world surrounding him than our civilized child to whom sound is more often a noise. It is only when we watch a blind person substitute auditory perception for vision that we realize the extent to which we could use our sense of hearing—a use that might be of the utmost help to the general maturation of the handicapped child whose perception of the world is bound to be incomplete.

Musical activities can help the handicapped child to use a number of mental processes connected with sound and movement—mental operations that are part of the learning process such as: memory—cognition—recognition—the apprehension of patterns of sounds and their discrimination—the interpretation of these patterns—the understanding of causes and effects related to the production of musical sounds—the power to relate sound to movement and to written symbols, and many others. At any level of intelligence music represents an experience of the mind. At the lowest end it can still help to develop the processes of automatism and imitation used in some simple musical activities suitable to the severely subnormal. At the other end, music can feed the intellectual hunger of an intelligent and musical child, and provide him with a truly rewarding and creative pursuit, as may be the case with children struck with polio or other forms of crippling diseases which do not affect the mind.

The development of intelligence depends on the consciousness of sensory experiences. In musical activities other senses than the auditory are involved, such as touch and sight, which produce awareness. Those are complementary to the process of hearing and could not function in music without some degree of auditory consciousness.

PLAYING AND SINGING

The sense of touch is one of the direct means through which the child explores the world and acquires conscious knowledge. Touching objects that interest us continues to be a spontaneous reflex in adult life, otherwise the notices 'Do not touch' would not be exhibited in public places. The manipulation of objects that have a definite function is of great help to children whose sense perception is restricted or deficient. In music there are many opportunities to touch, feel, and manipulate instruments; to look at them and to see how they are made; to use fingers, lips, or other parts of the body to produce a tone, and to get awareness and control.

The use of a musical instrument, however elementary or primitive, combines auditory, tactile, and visual perception. It requires motor control in time and space. If we conceive music as organized sounds we can say that performing music is the use of co-ordinated and controlled movement in relation to the musical pattern. This activity should help the child to form in his mind an image of the movement and to direct it, a mental process that is important in the physiotherapeutic treatment of cerebral palsy and other crippling diseases (see p. 120). The manipulation of an instrument includes a number of other mental processes such as the apprehension of the physical form of the instrument—of its nature—of the way it works, which always interest children. The sight of the vibration of a string or the feel of the resonance of a drum's skin can open to the child a world in which causes and effects can be perceived, provoked and tested, and are at the same time wonderful and logical. Even deaf children can be exposed to musical vibrations and respond to their rhythm.

A child who can make his instrument or participate in its making gains much insight into its manipulation and musical technique. He can understand and grasp why the instrument is made in a certain way and produces a certain tone. Any child can make or help to make a drum out of a tin, a pipe out of a bamboo—or even at a higher level assemble the different parts of a harpsichord. This craft work serves a double creative purpose when the instrument thus made becomes the child's means of self-expression. Because of the emotional motivation behind the making of an instrument, the teacher should ask from the child standards as high as possible. This may help the child to be critical of the quality of his work. The handicapped child afraid of failures or suffering from a sense of inferiority can gain from an intelligent self-appraisal of his own efforts in a field where enjoyment remains the keynote.

The mental processes involved in singing are similar to those required in the playing of a musical instrument. But the production of a child's voice is a natural and spontaneous act and does not demand the same reasoned and logical approach as in the handling of an instrument. Nevertheless, in singing the child becomes more and more conscious of his natural instrument, of the breathing process, of intonation, tone and articulation, of the memory of sounds and words. All this demands the same mental effort and attention as any other musical activity. The act of singing requires a logical use of the breathing and vocal apparatus controlled by the mind. A child whose breathing is defective or whose articulation is poor can become conscious of the physical process of filling his lungs and opening his chest, of the movements of lips and tongue necessary to pronounce certain words. He can feel the vibrations of his vocal chords through touching his throat. He can even become aware of a good body posture when he stands and sings.

Much of this training in perceptual and physical awareness can begin at the level of imitation and automatism. A child can first imitate the teacher's movements during the music lesson and acquire automatic reflexes without reasoning. Some subnormal children may never go further than this non-intellectual stage. But even so they may produce musical results as good as and even better than what they achieve in other fields, by rote and repetitive methods. The results they gain in music are to them particularly gratifying because this is a field in which something concrete and tangible can be achieved at a low standard of intelligence, but is at the same time emotional and enjoyable. The mental effort involved even at that low standard fulfils one of the needs that exist in every child for some achievement due to a mental effort.

LEARNING TO LISTEN

Even at a subnormal level, and whether the child listens to, composes or makes music, music is a mental discipline which needs order, attention, and control of the mind. The most elementary musical experiences or activities require the apprehension of or feeling for a sequence of sounds that make sense through a logical pattern. Intuitive processes play an essential part in music, probably because it is basically an emotion— and many children or adults just 'feel' music. But the listener who 'feels' music has already unconsciously absorbed and accepted a certain intellectual order in music, otherwise the music would have no meaning at all. A musically untrained subnormal child is quite able to realize that a musical sentence stopped before its logical end is not finished, and to experience a feeling of surprise, or humour. The intuitive and sensory experience of music is spontaneous. It can develop through a suitable training in the discrimination of sound.

From his earliest stage a child finds around him a world of sounds which he can perceive, explore, and interpret. Already in his cradle he is sensitive to sounds, to the opening of a door or to his mother's voice, whether she speaks or sings. (see p. 28). If she pats or rocks him at the same time, he will also experience a feeling of physical rhythm connected with the sounds. At an early stage he is able to recognize the sound of bells and their meaning or the chimes of the ice-cream man. He absorbs unconsciously the broadcast music that surrounds him. Because of this early disposition to assimilate sound and its meaning before the pre-verbal stage, he should be offered as soon as possible every means to develop his auditory sensibility and to become more and more aware of the multifarious sounds which are part of his environment, which can be exciting to explore.

The mother of a handicapped child should help towards this sensory development at home with very simple means. The child can realize that a little box filled with sand does not make the same sound as a similar box filled with nails, or that the sound made by a tumbler when it is hit is different from that made on a piece of wood. Little by little the child relates the sound with the object and the action and can name them. He may even discriminate and prefer certain sounds to others. This can be observed when the child tries to repeat sounds which he finds agreeable. In her excellent book, Miss Blocksidge describes the child's first steps in the exploration and discovery of sound that lead to auditory awareness. She advocates leaving the child alone, absorbed and undisturbed in his musical exploration of a sound-producing object, until he has matured enough to share his pleasure with others. She says:

These experiments in free music making are primarily intended to encourage the child to listen and to develop his listening faculty. This is of the foremost importance in the child's intellectual growth and not only useful as a means of music training.[1]

The handicapped child by reason of his disability may not find around him or may not be able to use the opportunity for such growth unless he is given the means and helped to experiment with sound, in which he may find a source of interest and enjoyment. Auditory awareness may lead him to become interested in music and to enjoy it.

The apprehension of music—or indeed of any language—depends essentially on memory—on the memory of the sound just heard in relation with the preceding and the following ones. The relationship of sounds through time and space gives meaning and expression to music. A young child experimenting with sounds may try to provoke and to repeat a relationship that he remembers as pleasing or exciting. This process may lead him to the appreciation of musical patterns of sounds related through rhythm, duration, and accentuation, and through the pitch of notes played separately or simultaneously. The apprehension of musical patterns rests on the power of

[1] K. M. Blocksidge, *Making Musical Apparatus and Instruments* (1957), p. 24.

attention of the listener, which is usually very weak in a handicapped child. Nevertheless a number of young children seem to memorize music without any mental effort and through a semi-conscious process. We are often surprised by the large repertoire of songs and musical ditties of youngsters supposed to be backward and inattentive.

The span of attention of a handicapped child is usually very limited, and this deficiency sets up a number of educational problems. In music as in other fields poor attention means poor listening. The teacher must find means through which the conscious attention of the child can be provoked and sustained long enough to make an impression on his mind and on his memory.

In music we have two ways of approaching this problem. One of them is the Gestalt method which may be suitable or not with a particular child. The Gestalt method is more often applied to visual processes, but it applies very well to music. A piece of music played through may at first make on the child's mind a general impression of 'feeling' without a definite structure, out of which he has probably picked up and remembered a few bits of melody and rhythms. If he can hear the piece often enough the emerging patterns he can perceive and recognize increase in number, fit together more and more, and in the end become a whole with shape, structure, and full meaning. This method is good only when the child is able to sustain his attention throughout the piece in order to detect, during the performance, the patterns which he can subsequently recognize, recall, anticipate, and remember. The music should be selected accordingly, since the child's mind has to be kept throughout in a state of alertness and expectation.

In many other cases the method should be based on a 'piecemeal' approach. For instance, when the child is volatile, hyperactive, and unable to fix his attention on the same object for more than a few seconds, then he should be made to listen to extremely short items, even to single sounds, within his span of attention, and significant enough to make an immediate effect on his mind. In the process the child may become aware of the basic elements of pitch—duration, intensity, or colour which are present in every musical sound and carry an expressive meaning. Little by little the child may perceive their relationship and become able to keep attentive for an increasing length of time. This technique is described in detail in Chapter Six.

The child learns to discriminate between musical sounds in the same way as he learns to discriminate between verbal sounds in language. He learns to understand speech through hearing people speak around him. He picks up a few sounds or words that little by little fit in a general sequence. He may be conscious of the general feeling of the sequence, before being conscious of the meaning of words, through the tone and intonation of the speaking voice. In the same way, he gets a general impression of a piece of music. In language he becomes increasingly conscious of certain syllables or words repeated to him piecemeal and which in the end, when added to one another, take a full meaning; and so he does with musical sounds and patterns.

Whatever the approach taken in his training towards music appreciation, music demands from the child the mental activity necessary to memorize and organize auditory perception, and the process should be developed to the utmost of the child's ability.

Listening to music can stimulate the child's mind by provoking mental associations and imagery related to his own experiences in life. The impact of the music depends on the child's imaginative power, on his ability to relate one experience to another and to integrate them. The development of imagery and mental association may be one of the greatest benefits a handicapped child can receive from listening to music, especially when the process can be directed towards creative and constructive aims in which mind and emotions are integrated. The process may consist of extremely simple experiences.

Simple musical sounds can be mentally evocative—not necessarily descriptive—of objects such as the sound of church bells—train whistles—the ticking of clocks—and many others that are within the child's experience. This effect of sound connected with things corresponds to the child's animistic conception of the world, since sound seems to give life to inanimate things.

When at all possible one should leave to the child himself the joy of discovering the meaning of sounds when he listens to music, and not prompt him to make certain associations that may seem exciting to an adult but have no value in themselves. These leave little mark on the child's mind. Neither is it very fruitful to give too many explanations about the piece or even to attach a full story to it, except with subnormal children. But even with those we should always remember that in any creative activity the value of the experience resides in what the child puts into it by himself without being prompted by an adult. I have often observed in handicapped children this joy of discovery in music, especially in those whose contacts with the world are severely limited. They experience a thrilling pleasure when they suddenly hear in the music, without having been prepared, something they can relate to their own experience, for instance when they recognize the tone of the bagpipes or the song of the cuckoo. In the same way a child who spontaneously recognizes a tune he knows experiences the pleasure that comes from familiarity and knowledge. Even at the infant or immature stage this pleasure is real and should be encouraged.

The world of animals is also related to music, where mice can squeak, cats miaow, butterflies flitter and fly, and hens peck—those and many others make a picture in the child's mind. There is also in music a world of people that is not so descriptive or imitative, but brings to the child's mind the image of a character through the mood of the piece—such as the 'Gay Farmer', the 'Old Beggar', or the 'Spanish Dancer'.

At a more intellectually mature stage the child can associate music with a broader world in which music is truly evocative of countries or landscapes and that stimulate the child's imaginative process, pieces such as *Fingal's Cave* by Mendelssohn, *Vltava* by Smetana, *The Sunken Cathedral* by Debussy; also pieces related to natural phenomena such as the Storm in Beethoven's Pastoral Symphony, or 'Sea Interludes' by Benjamin Britten.

The handicapped child who for physical, emotional, or intellectual reasons is not able to communicate with the world at large can be helped by music to broaden and illuminate his restricted conception of the world—a world that may become more real through his imagination stirred up by an experience that can be repeated again and again. Music relates to history, geography, nature and science, and to writing and reading, to free composition and many other pursuits of the mind. This close relationship has led me to make a number of experiments with subnormal children on the assumption that the emotional impact of music stimulates the child's mental activity and develops the learning process.

A musical experience makes different impressions on the child's mind. The sensuous pleasure given by agreeable sounds is non-intellectual, but more children than one thinks are able to feel the musical form and derive satisfaction from the logical organization of sounds which appeals to their sense of order in things of the mind. A musical phrase abruptly stopped in the middle makes even an E.S.N. child laugh because it feels humorous or silly and he knows that something is wrong.

MAKING UP TUNES

Any child, consciously or not, is sensitive to intellectual order such as exists in music, an order that may help him to feel secure, to channel and stabilize his emotions. When a child tries to make up a tune he usually attempts to put it into a form that gives meaning—although the result may be very far from an adult's conception of musical form.

In some cases, especially when a handicapped child is not able to verbalize, he may find it easier to make up a tune with the teacher's help. On the whole making up a tune and picking up the notes on a keyboard requires a mental process much more simple than trying to build up words into sentences. Our Western music is made of a basic number of seven notes, and even three of them are enough to compose a tune that makes sense. Most children have been exposed to so much broadcast music that they possess a feeling for some kind of intelligent use of the sounds. This helps them when they attempt to make up simple tunes, although they have to submit to a certain amount of mental discipline in the process. Here again the mind and the emotions are closely interwoven, they enrich and stimulate one another as in any other form of creative activity. When an inarticulate child finds a way to express himself and communicate through his own little tunes he may become more aware of his own personality.

The pentatonic scale is musically and intellectually the easiest sequence of notes to be used in the first attempts. This scale corresponds to the series of black keys on the piano and does not present any challenge to the mind. The notes can be arranged in any order, and whatever the order, always sound harmonious. Thus the child's imagination is not fettered by the laws governing other scales and the result of his work on a pentatonic scale is always acceptable. This is an important consideration with immature children whose need is to produce an immediate result and are not mature enough to project their musical effort towards the future (see p. 30).

When a school is preparing a musical show, the children sometimes join together to make up tunes for the occasion. I have seen a number of schools for physically handicapped children and E.S.N. schools engaged in such very fruitful enterprises. The children benefit greatly from pooling together their mental efforts towards a communal undertaking which gives them an opportunity to make their own suggestions, to offer or to receive criticisms. They are willing to accept the mental discipline necessary to the success of the scheme. In the process the music teacher may discover among the group a child who possesses musical aptitude likely to develop. Any group of handicapped children can participate in such musical activities, provided that the music teacher selects the children who can be stimulated and stimulate one another in the process.

READING MUSIC

The child who makes up a tune is probably not yet able to write it down, and the teacher does it for him. This can stir up the child's interest in musical notation. I have observed that children, especially those who have reading difficulties, are fascinated by musical notation. The teacher should encourage any desire to understand musical symbols which may motivate the child to learn musical writing. This interest shown by the child is a further step in his musical and general maturation and may lead to a number of developments.

When a child can write down and read his musical compositions he is able to keep and to compare them; he may wish to improve from one to another. He may contribute as an individual to the school activities; he may get kudos at home and among his friends. This satisfaction can help him to integrate better, especially during the difficult periods when any individual skill or achievement takes special significance.

Reading music requires a mental process which translates written symbols into musical sounds. The child at the very elementary stage may be able to relate sounds and symbols by rote or automatism. A subnormal child may achieve reading music in the same way. Some children who have no mental ear connect a written musical sign to a concrete place on the keyboard or a hole in the pipe. But past that elementary stage musical notation is very complex: each symbol represents the relative duration and pitch of the note and is written on a five-line stave, horizontally for a sequence of notes, vertically for simultaneous sounds. Some handicapped children may never be able to use their eyes in this double direction, let alone the mental interpretation of the signs. If in doubt, it is advisable to start the child on a monodic instrument before assessing the child's aptitude for reading music. Inability to read music may be a stumbling-block and frustrating to an otherwise musical child. This inability is an impediment that impairs or stops the musical progress of the child, however skilful or even impressive he may be in making up for the deficiency, in the same way as the child's inability to read impairs his general education. Nevertheless in jazz, which requires a special gift of improvisation by ear and manipulative skill on the instrument, reading musical notation is not essential. There are also children whose particular musical memory, together with a specific keyboard skill, enables them to give on the piano an approximate rendering of music they have heard. This is a precious gift that gives much pleasure. But the performance is generally sketchy and distorted because of the child's lack of musical training and mental discipline. He is usually not able to play with others and to submit to the necessary order.

Reading or writing music requires discipline of the mind. It also requires some essential knowledge of the theory of music that deals with the logical relationship between musical sounds through their pitch and duration. This study may help the child to understand the concept of numbers since it involves the solution of problems such as adding, subtracting, and multiplying; and decimals, based on sound as a unit of time.

Many music teachers are afraid that the mental effort involved may put off the child and they try to sugar the pill or to avoid the subject. They probably have been bored by their own teacher and want to stay on the safe side, especially when they realize how much music can mean to a handicapped child. But if the subject is presented with imagination as an interesting pursuit in itself the child may become 'enthusiastic' —such as a little dwarf in a school for physically handicapped children who said he was going to do well in the examination in theory of music because he was so enthusiastic about the subject.[2]

STUDYING MUSIC

A musical child may follow up with the study of harmony; that is, the art of musical chords and the relationship of musical parts. Harmony, being a more intellectual subject, should be taken up only by a musical child whose mind can mature. It may lead him to compose seriously, an absorbing and creative pursuit suitable to a homebound child left to himself who may suffer from solitude. Moreover, his music may give pleasure to others, in which he is the giver and not the recipient.

[2] Geoffrey Smales, paper on 'Music with Physically Handicapped Children', London Conference, Society for Music Therapy and Remedial Music, 1960.

The study of music does not consist only in the acquisition of purely musical skills, performing, composing, or appreciating music. A child can also become interested in the history of music; in the way music has been part of people's lives; in the life of the composers whose music they enjoy. The life of Mozart can be vivid to a child's mind, and so are many stories about Handel's childhood, Mozart's family life, or Paganini's dream. In a hospital for cerebral palsied children[3] some of them eagerly tried to tell me some facts they remembered about Beethoven's life and his walks in the country. Their knowledge increased the effect made on them by the storm in the Pastoral Symphony.

Many handicapped children taught with imagination display a great interest in the history of music which can help towards their mental development, since it opens to some of them windows on the past or present world. The lives of the great composers may become to the handicapped child something more than a series of anecdotes. Through their music they are to the more mature child real people whose lives can be inspiring because so many of them faced with courage a difficult life.

The intellectual appeal of music contains many emotional factors which are particularly suitable to the handicapped child. Indeed music may be called an adventure of the mind in which intellect and emotion cannot be dissociated.

[3] J. Alvin, 'Music in the Wards', Society for Music Therapy and Remedial Music, 1958.

4

SOCIAL MATURATION

MUSIC is the most social of all arts. It creates communication between people in infinite ways, since musical experiences are based on joined activities—even in an indirect way when a lonely listener enjoys the recorded performance of a group of players. Interpersonal relations take place when people share the same musical experience, either when they listen to music together or when they make music together.

To most people the obvious form of a social music group is a physically active one in which every member aims at a common result and makes his own vocal or instrumental contribution. I propose to discuss the music group in terms of social maturation, and to show how musical activities can help towards the social development of the handicapped child.

The social integration of the child starts in the family circle, which is the first social group to which he belongs. This is followed by social integration in the larger world of the school, in groups of increasing numbers. In special schools the numbers are kept as low as possible, not only for educational reasons, but because a handicapped child has many problems of social integration that he cannot solve within a large group. It is essential for a handicapped child to gain and develop social awareness in order to become an accepted member of any group in spite of his handicap.

IN THE FAMILY

The presence of a handicapped child often disrupts the unity of the family and creates problems of relationship and integration. The handicapped child, being necessarily dependent, is too often within the family the recipient, the spectator, or even the outsider. There should be in the family circle some ways in which the child could get some personal success and contribute something of his own to the family life.

I have met not many but inspiring instances in which music had become a shared and creative activity between the mother and the handicapped child. Curiously enough the two cases I should like to quote are very similar but have taken place very far apart on the two sides of the Atlantic.

In each case the child was subnormal, but normally responsive to music. The mothers longed for a relationship with the child at a higher level than material, something through which the child could make some contribution to the home life. The mothers had never studied music seriously, but each of them possessed a good aptitude and they began to take music lessons and practised hard. One of them learnt the recorder, the other the piano, in which they became quite proficient. A little later each of the mothers began to teach her child under the guidance of a music therapist, and each child made good progress. The influence on the family life in each case was quite striking. First the mother-child relationship had been transformed. The mother, unexpectedly, had become the recipient. She owed to the child and acknowledged that she had achieved through him a precious individual means of self-expression that she greatly enjoyed and was appreciated by her husband. Then she was able to communicate with the child at a cultural level and could help him towards some kind of achievement. Since none of his brothers and sisters learnt music the child's success in his own field gave him a special place in the family circle and helped him to develop self-confidence. If he could not read, he could play.

When the family supports the handicapped child's musical efforts and understands the tremendous value it may have for him throughout his deprived life, the consequences can be far-reaching. The music teacher of a school for physically handicapped children has been able to persuade several parents to buy a piano for their children who had become quite proficient and were then able to derive great pleasure from making music for or with friends at home. The possession of a piano may transform the home life of a housebound cripple who is too often a lonely spectator in this age of radio and television and lacks more than any disabled person some creative means of activity he can share with others,[1] and through which he may become a useful and popular member of a group.

IN THE SCHOOL AND TRAINING CENTRE

A handicapped child may be more aware of his disability among the members of his family circle than in a special school or a centre where every child is similarly affected. The school should be to him a community of which he is a member, where similar problems have to be faced and may be solved; a community where his social sense can be awakened and developed through various kinds of human relationships; a group in which he has to give as much as to receive. The school from the beginning is a world of his own, different from the family circle, in which larger groups exist that impose on him certain patterns of behaviour to which he is trained to conform. One of these is the music group.

A group is an association of individuals who cannot integrate unless each of them is aware of himself even before being aware of others (see p. 26). We have described the growth of musical awareness through the perceptual exploration of sound. This musical development follows a chronological pattern that, as we have shown, may be upset or distorted by a handicap, namely a perceptual, emotional, or mental disorder. The child should first pass through the stage of individual musical experiments before joining a musical group, in order to gain the necessary self-consciousness which in music and personality development grow simultaneously. He should be able to produce or reproduce sounds on a simple instrument or to direct his voice. He should be aware that a specific movement requires a certain space, a feeling that should develop when he stands or sits among others who also require space to sing or to play. The considerate use of space is part of good musical training in a group as well as good social behaviour. In order to do this the child has to become physically aware of others, a kind of spatial awareness that is often deficient in the psychotic or in the cerebral palsied child.

[1] Geoffrey Smales, 'Music with Physically Handicapped Children', paper read at Conference of the Society for Music Therapy and Remedial Music, Leeds, 1963.

Many handicapped children lack the self-awareness or awareness of others that is indispensable to social integration and stay too long at the stage of egocentricity, when the rest of the world does not seem to exist. For these children music can be truly therapeutic. Music is made of sounds that envelop the child and against which he is defenceless, making him aware of a world of auditory perception in which he can eventually participate and then join others. This process may create communication and consciousness in the deeply disturbed—or in the anti-social child.

Once the child has become conscious that he himself is producing sounds that are his own and that he can do so at will, he is musically ready to join a music group and learn how to behave musically and socially within the group. At the right stage a suitable music group can provide a sheltered and pleasant situation in which at the same time infantile behaviour is not acceptable, since each of its members is an individual, responsible for his own part and towards the whole, musically as well as socially. We have discussed how, even at the infant stage, a music-making group may offer the handicapped child a sheltered situation in which he feels secure (see p. 28). But when the child is immature or has emotional difficulties, he may feel too exposed in the music group. For instance, this may happen with a child suffering from shyness, or a sense of inferiority or lack of self-confidence.

There are various ways of dealing with the situation, and the essential is to give the child self-confidence in his musical ability first by himself or with another child, and then with a group. He may be motivated by curiosity or interest to join others, a motivation that can help to break his self-defence mechanism. I myself have observed this a number of times, especially with children who are afraid of words. Then the appeal comes from the attraction of a musical experience itself and not from words from the teacher. This happened during a demonstration that I was conducting in a fairly large hall with a group of mentally retarded children who were between seven and twelve years old. The audience was numerous and included teachers, psychologists, psychiatrists, and the parents who had brought their children. Most of the children followed me readily on to the stage, mounting the steps from the floor. They were attracted by the 'cello case I had just promised to open. Only one small girl refused to join. She continued to cry and cling to her mother. The mother then sat with her in the first row of the audience and the demonstration started on the stage. After a few moments the little girl was so enthralled by what was happening there that she left her mother, came up by herself, and sat quietly on a chair left vacant among the other children. She co-operated without any difficulty and experienced much happiness throughout the rest of the demonstration.

Every child is attracted by a music group, and even more so when he can join in order to make music himself. Even at the play stage there are certain rules that the child should follow, provided he has absorbed some concepts of a code of behaviour; he should be willing to be shown how to use his instrument in order to produce a pleasing tone, how and where to stand when he sings with others. Some well-meaning parents or teachers try to make a child join a music-making group before he is ready to co-operate, and he is unlikely to benefit from the experience; or he may disturb the group; or adopt the wrong attitude towards making music. But when he has acquired some individual skill at singing or handling a little instrument, the achievement may motivate him to join a group and to integrate.

Unless the teacher is so permissive that the child making music in a group is allowed to be wrapped in himself and unaware of others, he is bound to become musically conscious of the group. In a choir he cannot ignore the other members of the group standing near, whose voices are so audible that the words they say or the mistakes they make can be detected at once by their neighbours. In an instrumental ensemble children are quick to perceive who does well or badly, provided that the teacher's method aims at producing a musical tone and not a noise in which parts cannot be discerned. In the latter case it becomes unsocial music-making.

The place or part in the group allotted to each individual

child is of great importance since it affects the group as a whole. In a group of handicapped children each of them is different, with different needs to be catered for and different problems to be solved. The management of the group can be truly therapeutic, irrespective of the child's musical aptitude, if the music teacher possesses the necessary skill and insight. A child can be put, physically or musically, in front or at the back of the group; he may be given full responsibility for a part or share it with another child. He may be asked to conduct the group, to march in front or to follow at the rear. He may have to accept another child's superiority or to tolerate his mistakes. He may be asked to help others who cannot manage unaided or accept help willingly when needed.

The child who possesses acquired or natural auditory discrimination is able to recognize and follow certain parts in which he has to fit his own, even, at the most simple, to imitate or repeat a rhythm; he may have to keep silent when others play, or play when others keep silent; he may play a part in unison with another child, and the two children have to co-operate and play the same passage in the same way. All these processes happen at the most elementary stage of music-making, and the child in the group should become more and more conscious of the musical and the personal relationships involved. The musical behaviour to which the child has to conform, self-control, tolerance, and acceptance, is part of social behaviour generally. This remains true whether the group is a small infant percussion band, a junior or senior school choir, or a symphonic orchestra of experienced performers.

No group can function unless its members are attentive and able to sustain their attention. The problem of attention is common to all handicapped children. But making music is an emotional outlet and a physical activity at the same time, and the two factors combine to hold the child's interest and attention.

The child who integrates in a small music group can transfer this integration to larger social groups. Several of my pupils who suffered from emotional disturbance and had difficulty in adjusting themselves socially found their way towards integration and stability through their music group at the primary stage. When some of them had to enter the secondary school, which seemed to them a frightening experience, they were able to join the school orchestra. This offered them a familiar, secure, and even protective situation through which they integrated with their new surroundings and felt at once needed. The same observations can be applied to the school choir, which is a socially integrating force in any type of school, and the effect of which may go far beyond the value of musical achievement.

It is the group, not the individual, that is presented with a musical goal, and this emphasis creates strong feelings between the group and the individual. The unadventurous or shy child may become ambitious for the group's success to which he contributes inconspicuously. The handicapped child may have little hope of individual achievement in music and therefore little ambition, but his contribution to a successful group may be a substitute. The music teacher should thus set the aim as high as possible in order to obtain from each participant the maximum effort towards the common goal. This effort can bring the child great satisfaction and reward. Some special schools enter music festivals for choral or instrumental groups, and a number of them gain awards on the same standard as normal schools—a source of pride and happiness not only to each of the members of the music group but also to the school as a community.

Irrespective of the level of performance the music group can provide either a sheltered situation run on a permissive basis —or a situation in which discipline is imposed. Whatever the case, a music group should create free and happy enjoyment mixed with the acceptance of musical rules that have social significance. The musical result always should be as good as the child's handicap permits, and one should not forget that the child is making 'music'. It should accordingly never be allowed to degenerate into noise and disorder. There are many other non-musical activities in which noise and uncontrolled behaviour can provoke an emotional outlet if so desired. But there is no reason why musical activities should degenerate into senseless noise, create in the child an attitude destructive of music and provoke what is just bad musical behaviour. Self-control especially in the volume of tone is the proof that the child has consideration for the others' parts and that he feels part of the group. Wall's remarks on the social adjustment of the child do not refer specially to music but fit in here in the most appropriate way:

The child has to learn to respect the rights of others and to conform to exigencies which are often contrary to his egoistic desires; he should come steadily more and more and in increasingly complex ways to experience and discriminate between situations in which he must abandon or modify a desire of his own in order to conform to the life of a group and others where he must defend his own rights.[2]

IN ADOLESCENCE

So far we have discussed the integration in a music group of the young and the junior handicapped child. When he enters the period of adolescence the changes that occur in his social attitudes may affect his attitude towards the music group, and correspond to the change in his feelings towards music. Methods suitable for a group of younger children do not satisfy adolescents. Another orientation and significance should be given to the music group. It should become more than a self-contained unit, helping the handicapped child to project himself towards the outside world.

This gradual social maturation of the group which corresponds to its musical maturation is used in a residential school for blind children.[3] At that school the very young children start by making music for their own sake and enjoyment. In the second stage they become integrated and conscious of the group, the choir then contributes to the inner life of the school. Later on this choir, which is musically good, goes out to sing and to entertain old or sick people in homes or hospitals. The group is then performing an act of social service of the greatest

[2] W. D. Wall, *Education and Mental Health* (4th. ed. 1960), p. 60.
[3] K. M. Brunton, 'The Blind Child', paper read at Conference of the Society for Music Therapy and Remedial Music, Leeds, 1963.

value to them and to the beneficiaries. These blind children mature socially and musically through three stages, first making music for themselves, then with others, and then for others.

Such an ideal can be reached with intelligent blind children whose auditory and musical sense can be highly developed—it may not be possible to achieve such a social and musical standard with other types of handicapped children. Nevertheless at the adolescent stage the school choir should be made to carry increasing responsibility and given a growing importance in school functions and shows, and this applies to the instrumental ensemble as well, if it is at all acceptable musically.

The handicapped school-leaver who has enjoyed music throughout his school life should not feel that when he leaves school he will find no more opportunities for musical association. In fact, the handicapped adolescent has normal social needs and fewer means to fulfil them. Some E.S.N. schools follow their work of social integration through a club for school-leavers attached to the school, and link their musical activities to those of the school to provide a valuable and secure transition at a difficult period for the handicapped youth who feels as Wheeler says 'an intense desire for group membership. There is a strong urge towards co-operation with other adolescents, and there is a great possibility of developing group-loyalties in the pursuit of common ends.'[4]

The youth at that time who leaves the sheltered life of the school may experience the same difficulty in adjusting socially as the young child who leaves the security of his home for the unknown world of the school.

The child who grows up wants to choose his own friends on the basis of similar tastes. In adult life this similarity creates understanding and companionship more than similarity of occupation. We should try to open in the life of the handicapped child as many channels as possible to give him chances to associate with his peers, and to join groups that share his tastes. But in order to do so he may have to discard childlike musical activities that are no longer suitable and become part

[4] *Mental Health and Education* (1961), p. 107.

of a more socially mature music group. In an orthopaedic hospital where ensembles of bamboo pipes and wind instruments have a real therapeutic value with the crippled children, the adolescents are invited to join the teachers and staff music group and play with them at their adult level.

If it happens that an adolescent shows signs of interest in some type of music he should be given, whenever possible and in good time, instruction which will enable him to join later on a music-making group of his own liking—for instance, a guitar group—or which will allow him to cultivate an interest shared with others, such as listening to recorded music. In some progressive schools for handicapped children the older pupils are encouraged to organize freely their own music group and they develop initiative and purposeful co-operation in the process.

LISTENING TO MUSIC TOGETHER

The preceding pages apply chiefly to the music-making group in which the child is physically active. But there is another way through which music is also a shared experience of great social value, and that is the music-listening group. The same processes of social integration are involved but in a more subtle and emotional form. These processes may work below or above the ego level, since listening to music may stir up primitive instincts or lead to sublimation. As in the music-making group, listening to music together provokes in children a number of personal interrelationships because they are sharing an experience, and may remember it for a long time. Shared memories are associations that can link people together and give them a sense of companionship and belonging throughout life.

In order to listen attentively the children should share the right attitude towards a musical performance, respecting each other's pleasure and not disturbing the group.[5] In schools for normal children we have sometimes met teachers who are too

[5] In Britain this training could start at the stage of 'Listen with Mother', the BBC programme for the under-fives.

much concerned about the social behaviour of children listening to a live performance, and not enough about the pleasure the child may experience, a pleasure that should make him behave well and control himself.

In special schools the attitude of the teaching staff is different: they are more concerned about the way the children will react to the music and wonder whether they will enjoy it. But I have observed that, even in schools for disturbed teenagers, interest and sustained enjoyment can help to provoke good social behaviour in the group, in spite of the pessimistic outlook of the staff. Even in a short performance interest and enjoyment can be contagious and help to integrate the group.

A music-listening group is, if only for a short time, a small community in which the child's personality can be adjusted and directed, and in which each of the children participates —there are good or bad listeners who can affect the whole group. The effect of the group on the child is quite obvious: no child unless he is very mature could listen as attentively and for such a relatively long period if he was alone in the room with the performer. I have tested this fact on musical children who in any case enjoyed the music, but who were obviously happier and more concentrated in a group sharing their pleasure and often their enthusiasm. The influence of the group can be favourable or adverse in any experience. Enthusiasm or boredom spreads equally well from one child to another. There are leaders in any group who set the atmosphere for good or bad social behaviour: they should be watched and placed accordingly.

A group of children integrates more readily and easily during a live performance when the musician can adapt his musical and psychological approach to the general and individual needs of the children. It is much more difficult to achieve this integration with a recorded or televised performance which is planned for a great number of different groups and cannot be adapted at the time to the reaction of a specific group. Moreover, there is no personal contact between the child and the performer, a contact particularly important to the handicapped child, and a programme planned for normal children may not be suitable for the handicapped, whose sense perception is often impaired. For instance, children suffering from mental retardation do not perceive easily music played at a normal speed—recorded music is sometimes, for the sake of brilliance, faster than was the live performance. Many of the E.S.N. children I have trained in music appreciation and discrimination find that even the pieces familiar to them are too fast on the radio. When I took them to a concert in a hall the same children who were such good listeners in their own group at school could not follow and were overwhelmed. They could not integrate in a larger unit and share with normal children in the concert hall. The most difficult task for a performing musician is to make a true listening group of a number of handicapped children of very different chronological or mental ages—a situation that I have sometimes met in special schools. The handicapped child at school first belongs to a small group, his own form, and may not be ready to integrate into a larger unit. Unless this is taken into consideration in planning performances of music in a special school, some children may miss the social benefit that a suitable group could give them, and they may also not behave well.

The live performances of music that are invaluable to the child's musical and social training can be the first step towards the appreciation of recorded music. Lessons in music appreciation can be shared by the children in the same way as all other musical activities. Since they relate to the whole field of musical form and expression they can become a serious group study and lead to the composition of music by groups of children. Some special schools plan group projects based on the programme of the music appreciation class, in which each child makes his contribution to the whole. Musical experiences can affect or help to form other groups. For instance, a music group that I was training in an E.S.N. school joined together to make up books of various cuttings related to the music, which they collected with great care. They wanted to bind these books which were very precious to them. A class was then formed to teach them binding in order to do so—and binding has become one of the best group activities of the school.

CONCLUSION

A child who has enjoyed a music-listening group, handled from the start in a way in which pleasure and enjoyment are mixed with social awareness and consideration for others, is ready to join other groups of listeners—even if he cannot perform himself. Music can be at any age and stage a world in which people share the same tastes and the same pleasures, irrespective of social status, intelligence or education—an all-important consideration with regard to the handicapped child eager to communicate and to share experiences, at the same level, with normal people. Beethoven, Stravinsky, Verdi, Gershwin, and others speak equally to audiences of people who vary much physically, mentally, and emotionally but who become an integrated group during a performance. Any handicapped child, adolescent, or adult should be given opportunities to attend concerts—or to become a member of a gramophone club in which choosing the music, listening, and discussing together create a valuable link between the members of the group—irrespective of the type of the music chosen. In this way, as in many others, music may make its contribution to the social development of the handicapped child towards an integrated life.

5

THE MENTALLY SUBNORMAL CHILD

MAKING MUSIC

DEGREES OF SUBNORMALITY

The subnormal child has been the subject of much attention, study, and research. Educationists, psychologists, teachers, and doctors have become more and more aware that such a child needs special methods of education and treatment in order to grow into a useful and acceptable member of the community. Subnormality may come from endogenous causes such as cerebral lesion, maldevelopment, or a perceptual disability, or from extragenous causes such as illness, poor home conditions, or some emotional disturbance that has created an emotional blockage.

The mental limitations of the backward child are measured in terms of time. The gap between his chronological age and his mental age increases until he reaches adulthood and cannot develop any more. Degrees of mental retardation vary from the dull child down to the imbecile, and these degrees are imperceptibly different. The dull child is one whose mind when stimulated may catch up—the mind of a child diagnosed as 'subnormal' rarely does. The educationally subnormal child (E.S.N.) develops at from half to three-quarters of the rate of a normal child—the development of a severely subnormal child (S.S.N.) may be as low as one quarter of a normal child or even lower. There are no clear qualitative or quantitative lines between the deviations produced by mental retardation. The child suffers from a light or severe, from a general or specific, impediment to his learning process.

Retardation is often made worse by emotional factors; many retarded children suffer from social or emotional maladjustment. Intellectual confusion prevents the child from adjusting to family or school life. He becomes more and more aware of his failures, especially when he is in a position to compare his achievements to others. He may become puzzled, bewildered, and give up any attempt that seems to him useless—he often exhibits the well-known compensatory reactions, ending in anti-social, unacceptable behaviour. Then his emotional state increases his learning difficulties.

Educationally subnormal children form by far the largest group of retarded children. They are catered for, as far as possible, in special schools or remedial classes. The E.S.N. child is able, at varying degree, to achieve some academic skills such as the three Rs. Given adequate training the E.S.N. adult should be able to get regular work. But this is increasingly difficult in an era of industrial automation.

The child in the group below the E.S.N. learns only by rote and automatism and cannot acquire academic skills. He possesses limited speech, but can usually be trained in physical and social habits. He is not fit for formal education and is catered for in training centres, where he can develop through various activities at his level. He will be dependent all his life and in need of economic support.

The lowest grade of severely subnormal child is totally dependent, cannot acquire good habits, and cannot integrate socially. He usually spends his life in an institution.

MUSIC AND THE SUBNORMAL CHILD

The effect of music on all types of subnormal children has been observed again and again. Itard mentions that his wild boy of Aveyron was responsive to musical sounds.[1] More recently Wall states that 'Many of the subnormals and all the dulls are capable of enjoying many of the more purely cultural aspects of their education, music, art, acting, dancing, for example.'[2] Carlson and Ginglend remark that 'a child who is singing or listening to music with others who enjoy it is surrounded by joy, in a sense "wrapped up in his music". . . . A retarded child easily becomes "enraptured" by simple melodious tunes. This general feeling for music is contagious. It

[1] L. Malson, *Les Enfants sauvages* (1964), p. 67.
[2] W. D. Wall, *Education and Mental Health* (1959), p. 222.

often reaches the spirit of the retarded child long before anything else reaches him.'[3] And also add that the very severely retarded child may be absorbing more through music than his responses reveal. But in spite of these observations there should be no undue optimism on the musical aptitude of the subnormal child. Burt is of the opinion that some school teachers 'often declare that dull or defective individuals are quite equal to the normal in musical appreciation. . . . My own experience is that, as in hand work, so in music, the capacities of the dull and defective appear unusually high only in comparison with their own performance in more academic subjects: rarely are they as good as those of a normal child of the same age.'[4]

THE RIGHT APPROACH

The value of music to a subnormal child resides in the fact that it can be treated as a non-academic subject at different levels of intelligence. We should consider music as a help to his general development, not in terms of musical achievement, since his deficiency will prevent him from rising above a certain standard. This applies even more to the severely subnormal who lacks reasoning power and cannot project himself into a future which is not immediate; a child who often has no speech and no means of communication but can respond to musical stimuli. Methods and uses of music can be adapted to all degrees of subnormality; it is possible to do a certain amount of teaching at low brain level and to make use of the mental ability, however poor, that the retarded child possesses.

The subnormal child needs creative experiences in which he can enjoy some relative success and through which he may develop. Tansley and Gulliford believe that 'the freedom and satisfaction of creative expression are often the means by which the child achieves balance and harmony in his own process of growth, and the child who achieves that, even partially is more able and ready to learn'.[5]

[3] B. W. Carlson and D. R. Ginglend, *Play Activities for the Retarded Child* (1961), p. 160.
[4] Sir Cyril Burt, *The Backward Child* (1951), footnote on p. 238.
[5] A. E. Tansley and R. Gulliford, *The Education of Slow Learning Children* (1960), p. 167.

Moreover, the subnormal child suffering from emotional instability often lacks the feeling of purpose and achievement which is essential to mental health. We should help him, says Kirk, 'to experience as many successes as possible. Having set standards for him that are attainable, try to present the steps in the learning of each skill in such a way and at such a rate that he will feel some measure of success.'[6]

The very young child can be offered suitable material to explore the world of sound but the material should correspond to his actual stage of development. Kirk advocates giving the child materials whereby he can make his own music. Nevertheless

they should be of such a nature that effort will have to be put forth for success but they should not be so difficult that success is impossible. There would be little value in giving a mentally retarded child rattles to play with when he has long since passed through the stage when a rattle holds his interest. Materials that are too immature for him will be as much a detriment to good emotional adjustment as play materials that are too advanced.[7]

IN INFANCY

Music can be part of the life of the subnormal child at an early age. There are certain steps in his musical initiation that take place long before school age. This can already be done in the family circle and is advocated by Carlson and Ginglend:

Often the first means of communication with a retarded child is made through music. The mother sings to the baby in the crib or in her arms. . . . If the mother sings a song with simple motions the child may imitate the motions and so join in the 'singing' long before he can say a word. This joining in an activity with another person gives the child a sense of security, a feeling of belonging which can grow as he joins larger groups, the family, a group of neighbourhood children, and later perhaps a class.[8]

AT SCHOOL AND IN THE TRAINING CENTRE

The limited equipment of the mentally retarded child is not all negative. It includes a few positive factors on which the

[6] S. Kirk, M. B. Karnes, and W. D. Kirk, *You and Your Retarded Child* (1956), p. 69.
[7] op. cit., pp. 95–96.   [8] *Play Activities for the Retarded Child*, p. 159.

music teacher can build a music programme, provided that he starts at that positive low level and follows the child's pace. The mind of the retarded child is not warped as in the case of a mental illness: it is deficient; neither is a backward child regressed: he has simply not progressed normally. These two factors are important when we consider the child's mental limitations within which the music teacher has to work. We cannot call on resources that have never been and never will be there. Nevertheless, except at a very low level of deficiency, the retarded child is able to make concrete associations; he can learn through automatism and repetition, he may possess some visual or auditory imagination perhaps not yet awake but capable of development; he may have curiosity that could become interest; his span of attention can be developed through special techniques; he likes to do things, to touch and manipulate objects; and above all he can be motivated with the right methods. The fundamental asset of the music teacher's task with subnormal children was clearly expressed by Burt when he said: 'Pleasurable emotion tends to stamp in whatever it accompanies.'[9]

Moreover, a number of musical activities are suitable to an undeveloped or primitive mind. Many of them are logical in a concrete way and do not require a long-term memory. Much of the enjoyment of music can be non-intellectual at the elementary stage. It has been said that all children accept music first as an emotional experience. They let 'music return to its primitive condition, an evocation of spirits through the medium of pure sound—before subjecting it to a critical analysis. Of course the end product—knowing and enjoying music—only comes after the analysis has merged with the purely primitive enjoyment of sound for its own sake.'[10]

From that primitive enjoyment of sound at the most simple level we can offer the child musical experiences up to the level he is able to reach, although the end product may fall very short of what a normal child can achieve.

[9] *The Backward Child*, p. 534.
[10] M. B. Lloyd-Phillips, 'How Children Listen to Music', *Music in Education* (July 1962), p. 99.

Music appeals to the emotional life of the retarded child, a life that is not at all as barren as his intellectual life. A backward child may experience a great many impressions, feelings, and emotions. He is not able to utilize them because he lacks the intellectual organization that is needed to do so. His inner life may be richer than one supposes, but he cannot express it well in words. I have observed this inadequacy in verbal expression in most essays written by E.S.N. children, although they had displayed great enthusiasm at the time and had kept a lively memory of the music.[11]

Music can be to a retarded child a sound of joy and happiness in many ways, and give him the opportunity to express himself alone or with others. Even if music can stimulate him as a listener, an aspect that will be discussed at some length, making music is more exciting for immediate purposes. He is then doing something: singing, playing an instrument, or moving to music.

We should not forget that all aspects of music are complementary to one another. The oneness of music is based on 'a universal axiom that composing, performing and listening are basically the same act of being musical'.[12] Even in a school programme these diverse aspects of music cannot be dissociated. A subnormal or any other child cannot grow musically unless he is exposed to many varied musical experiences. Educationists should agree that in a school programme for subnormal children 'music should include not only singing but listening and moving to music and acquiring some simple ideas and information which are likely to sharpen interest and increase pleasure'.[13]

MAKING MUSIC AND READING

It is difficult to integrate in a group a number of subnormal children playing or singing together. They are at different stages of social, emotional, and mental development and a

[11] See 'Children's responses', pp. 15–24.
[12] Frank Howes, 'Rhythm and Man', Lecture in London Course on Music Therapy (June 1962).
[13] A. E. Tansley and R. Gulliford, op. cit., p. 183.

common musical standard is not easy to find. Moreover, mentally retarded children tend to be less flexible than others.[14] They seem to adjust to new situations much more slowly than the normal child and they find it difficult to change their behaviour pattern. The music teacher should take this fact into account, and try to create among the group the emotional climate in which the child can unbend easily. This is best done in the singing group or the choir. The activities should be based on the learning ability of the children. Most of them can learn songs by rote, imitation, and repetition and do not need to look at the text of the words or at the musical notation. Nevertheless older children may benefit if they are given a clearly printed music part through which they can associate the sounds with the written text and follow the shape of the melody. Even unconsciously they may get from it some idea of the written signs that express words or music. I have often noticed that subnormal children are fascinated by musical notation. Their teacher should make use of this attraction to explain in an imaginative way the musical symbols used in the song. Most of these children cannot go further than a rudimentary kind of music reading. But we should point out that any achievement in 'reading'—that is, in the interpretation of the written symbol—goes further than an intellectual success. Among the three Rs, reading is the achievement that gives any child a social status without which he feels inferior. In consequence even the little he can achieve when he tries to read music seems to him immensely important, provided that the music teacher presents it as such.

The subnormal child learns through much repetition. The drawback of repetitive methods is that they easily breed monotony and suppress mental effort. Repetitive methods applied to music can be very varied and need not be monotonous. The same tune may be used again and again with different words, or at different speeds, or with different intensities. The child likes the familiarity of the basic pattern, but he has to be attentive to any change or addition made to it.

[14] S. A. Kirk, M. B. Karnes, and W. D. Kirk, op. cit., pp. 70 and 116.

Music can also give meaning to single sounds or syllables repeated again and again to improve or correct pronunciation.

It has been noticed by many teachers that the repetition of a single syllable such as 'B' or 'Tap' has no meaning in itself. It has no movement and leads nowhere. But when a musical accompaniment is provided that places the sound in a succession of melodic or rhythmical relationships with the piano part, the syllable loses its feeling of emptiness, takes sense, and even possibly an emotional meaning. In many songs, we can find or introduce monotone repeated words that are part of a whole and which feel truly exciting. Some songs have been composed for remedial purposes in the correction of speech defects. They are attractive and enable the child to make the necessary effort.[15]

There are many growlers among subnormal children, and it is difficult to give them a place in the choir without disturbing the others.[16] But in the monotonous use of his voice when such a part can be found for him, the growler feels at ease, and so do the others. In time he may learn to pitch his voice and benefit from all that can be gained in this activity.

A subnormal child who has difficulty in pitching his voice or in vocalizing can be greatly helped by using a kazoo. This is a rudimentary unmusical instrument, but in blowing in his kazoo and trying to pitch his voice in order to produce a specific sound, the child has to use his lungs, his vocal apparatus, his tongue, and his lips; otherwise there will be no pitched sound. The experience is quite exciting, and the child may then become aware of the various physical functions involved in a process that can help him to use in a better way his speaking and singing voice.

Many subnormal children suffer from physical impediments that affect their voice, for instance adenoids, catarrh, bad posture, or defective breathing. Many good habits can be acquired through singing; and some defects can also be remedied in this pleasant situation where the child is willing to make an effort and to sustain it.

[15] John A. Harvey, *Articulation and Activity Songs*, Paxton & Co. Ltd.
[16] J. P. B. Dobbs, 'Music and the Backward Child', Conference on Music Therapy in the Education of the Child, London, 1960.

The backward child is usually physically awkward, he often stoops, cannot stand or sit erect. Altogether he lacks physical dignity. The music teacher can help him to improve his posture when he is singing. He should stand erect but relaxed, place his feet and hands in the right position, and open his chest. This helps him to get confidence in the way he projects his voice, especially when the choir performs in front of an audience.

The human voice is the natural instrument, and singing is a spontaneous action. But singing activities require some physical awareness and control. A child who sings, whose body and mind are in action, finds in this activity a powerful outlet and experiences great emotional satisfaction. The initial spontaneity of this form of self-expression has a non-intellectual character that is specially suitable to a mentally retarded child.

SUITABLE MUSIC

Songs for retarded children are not easy to find. They have to appeal to a child whose power of attention is severely limited; who can grasp only short verbal or musical sentences; whose chronological age does not correspond to his mental or emotional level. He is full of discrepancies and may reject babyish or childlike material although his own verbal ability is so very limited.[17] At the same time, he is a child who may want either stimulation or relaxation, a child who may be afraid, or shy or over-assertive.

In spite of the many variations in temperament, or in mental and physical ability, that are characteristic of subnormal children, the music teacher has to provide songs that are attractive to all the children in his group. He can always safely exploit to the full the pleasure that all subnormal children experience in repetitive processes. Any music with a repetitive rhythm appeals to them. It should first be straightforward. Later on syncopated rhythms may be introduced for the reason that some retarded children feel the musical pulse better when syncopated elements are present in a two or four beat. Refrains are very suitable because they are the repetitive

[17] J. P. B. Dobbs, op. cit.

element in many songs, and they may even consist of only one repeated syllable or word. Monotony can easily be avoided if the teacher introduces little by little a number of musical factors that motivate the child to make an effort and to be attentive. For instance, the same passage can be sung loud or soft in order to make an echoing or whispering effect; crescendo or diminuendo correspond to an effect of moving near or far; an accelerando or a ritenuto express increasing or decreasing speed of movement. These effects and many others are expressive of feelings familiar to the child, and when they are well adapted give life and personality to his interpretation of the music. These effects demand from the children a certain amount of control. When it is too difficult for them to make a contrast, they should be divided into two groups, sharing in turn the different effects. The advantage of this technique is that the children may memorize a song more easily because they have an opportunity to keep quiet and to hear other children singing it.

The meaning of the songs should be simple enough to allow the child to mind his pronunciation of certain consonants or words and to sing in time.

Whether he sings, plays an instrument, or listens to music, time is with the subnormal child a deciding factor in the way he can function. The retarded child as well as any other likes the feeling given by fast music, but a rapid tempo suitable to a normal child defeats him. The impression of speed or liveliness should be made by a clear-cut rhythm and a bright tone in pieces moving at a moderate speed, not faster than he can follow. Later on, from that stable basis, he can experience the thrilling pleasure of singing 'faster and faster'. Even on a one-syllable word the retarded child immensely enjoys doing this, and lets out steam in the process. Going slower and slower is much more difficult, but can be replaced by singing softer and softer.

Since the attention of these children can be provoked but not easily kept, it is much more beneficial for them to learn and enjoy a great number of various and extremely short songs, possibly using only one or two verses of each of them. It makes the music session more enjoyable, provokes discrimination and preferences between the songs, and can help to develop some critical sense. The task of providing such a repertoire is not easy. But among nursery rhymes, nonsense rhymes, and jingles we can find many suitable songs about animals, things, and people that are familiar to the child—sea shanties, dances, and so on.

It would be a mistake to give these children always lively and gay music. Many retarded children seem to have a reflective or contemplative side in their nature. They are touched by music expressing religious or spiritual feelings, peace or serenity, love or sadness. Among the songs that can answer these needs are negro spirituals, carols, and a number of traditional melodies. Sometimes great music by Bach or Handel makes on them a deep effect.

A good repertoire of songs can provide the retarded child with an unlimited number of experiences that jog at his mind and stimulate his imagination; that can make the apathetic come out of his indifference, help the unstable to stabilize and the withdrawn to communicate.[18]

PLAYING INSTRUMENTS

The teacher of retarded children is handling two main kinds of pupils: those who work in a painstaking, stubborn way, and those who are unwilling or unable to make a mental effort. Many of these children are conscious of their mental poverty and inadequacy. It is essential to give them in the right way some kind of challenge and to present them with a task slightly above their actual level of attainment. Most retarded children can respond to this in music if they feel that the teacher does not underrate or overrate their ability but trusts them to perform at a certain standard. Music even treated in a non-academic way should make some demands on the child. Singing makes on the child as few intellectual demands as possible, but playing an instrument is a more conscious process and has a more concrete value because it consists in the training for and the acquisition of a technical skill.

[18] J. P. B. Dobbs, op. cit.

The challenge offered by music can be directed towards the group or towards the individual. In choir work, the teacher sets up a general standard of achievement for the group. In instrumental work, the standard set is individual first. Each child plays his own instrument that he can see, touch, and manipulate. The process is conscious and requires a certain amount of observation, understanding, memory, and control. The skill and intelligence necessary to play a musical instrument vary immensely, according to the nature of the instrument, from the most elementary to the most complex one. There are very simple instruments of a primitive kind perfectly suitable for even severely mentally handicapped children. But however elementary these instruments are they should never be the kind of cheap toys that have no musical value whatsoever and cannot provide a real musical experience. There is a minimum standard for quality of tone and intonation that is found only in well-made material easily available today.

I have already discussed the value of instrumental playing in the development of sense perception even with children who are not physically handicapped. The future of the subnormal child very much depends on his manual ability, on his control of specific movements in time and space, on his power of attention focused on a certain object. These qualities can be awakened and developed in making music, because they are necessary to the handling and playing of a musical instrument. The music teacher should help the child to develop his manual skill through his interest in a musical technique. This word 'technique' associated with music often arouses the feeling that it may kill or spoil the child's enjoyment. From my experience, and unless the child is too immature to gain from it, the technical side of an instrument rather enhances the attraction of music. The attitude of the music teacher is often responsible for the active interest and care the child takes in his musical instrument. The musical field of the retarded child is limited by his deficiency; nevertheless there are a certain number of instruments he can learn to play. In addition there are certain things he can learn through playing music. An E.S.N. child is able to grasp that his musical instrument is a 'tool' which has a certain scope and limitations that cannot be altered and govern its proper use. The handling of a 'tool' according to its nature and to its use applies to a musical instrument as well as to any other. The child who absorbs the right attitude towards craft in music may carry on this attitude towards manual work into the workshop. Because of his slow development and the difficulty he has in changing his pattern of behaviour, the retarded child should be encouraged as early as possible to adopt a healthy attitude towards his various activities, including music and manual work. Music is particularly suitable because it brings so much enjoyment at the same time.

KINDS OF INSTRUMENTS

A musical instrument, even one as simple as a rhythm stick, makes specific technical demands on the child, and each instrument up to the most complex ones can be graded according to the degree of intelligence necessary to handle it.

At the most elementary level we find some percussion instruments that are pitchless, require only very simple movements of one hand, such as a small hollow wooden box to be hit with a beater, or some drums, or the maccara, the jingle bells, and castanets on a holder. Others require co-ordinated movements of the two hands, such as the rhythm sticks, the cymbals, and the drum. The tambourine and the triangle are more elaborate because one hand holds the instrument and the other does the beating. The technique of the chime bars is very adaptable and extensive. The child may use only one bar with one beater, or make more elaborate movements when he uses a whole range of notes; he may even use two beaters, one in each hand. This more complicated technique applies to other similar instruments which consist of a series of different notes out of which a choice is to be made, such as the dulcimer, the xylophone, and others.

When the child has to make his own pitched notes, he must possess a certain amount of auditory discrimination. The most simple instruments for that purpose are among those in which one blows. They also require breathing and finger control. The recorder is often too difficult for a retarded child because of the relative complexity of the finger work. Unfortunately there does not seem to exist on the market an elementary wind instrument with a pure, musical tone, simple enough for a retarded child. He could use a bamboo pipe, but those have to be made by the child himself, and most retarded children could not do it.

Up the scale of suitable instruments played with the mouth is the harmonica, the bugle, and even the trumpet that a few backward youths seem to be able to tackle in some way.

Only very few retarded children, if any, would be able to learn to play a stringed instrument with a bow. The great difficulty in the technique of the violin and similar instruments is due to the two different tasks to be performed respectively by the left and the right hand. This produces a diversity of movements that subnormal children cannot co-ordinate. But there are ways of adapting the technique of these instruments for the use of subnormal children. This technique is rewarding only to the young or very backward children who would not be aware that they are using the instrument in a childlike manner, unless it can be done in connexion with a band. In that case it serves an adultlike and excellent purpose.

The most childlike way of playing on a violin or a 'cello is to use the bow on open strings only, if the child can manage to hold the instrument and control the movement of the bow. He can also not use the bow at all and pluck the open strings. The instrument should have only the number of strings he can manage—perhaps even only one—and the number can be increased when the child becomes more skilful. One cannot expect a retarded child to manage the complex technique of the left hand on the strings.

The guitar is an elaborate instrument because of the number of strings and the complexity of the fingering. Nevertheless with a powerful motivation, some retarded youths can more or less master two or three basic chords that are very useful in the accompaniment of songs or in an ensemble. The auto-harp can serve the same purpose with severely retarded children because the chords are made automatically by a bar pressing on the strings.

A great number of retarded children can memorize tunes easily and experience great joy in finding them on an instrument. The piano keyboard is a good field of exploration for that purpose. But after the first free exploratory stage, this recognition of a tune on the keyboard should become constructive and purposeful, otherwise the child's interest may disappear. Individual help there is needed. Most of the time the child plays with one finger, and although he may manage surprisingly well to find the right sequence of notes, he is usually quite inaccurate with regard to rhythm. Singing the tune at the same time makes him co-ordinate the whole process and helps him to bring rhythm into it. Children can also recognize or make up tunes on other instruments such as the chime bars, the dulcimer, or the auto-harp.

Most retarded children will, however, not be able to play the piano, unless they have enough physical and musical aptitude and patience. Nevertheless I have seen mongoloid children play with a good elementary technique some very simple piano pieces. This was the result of very experienced teaching, graded through slow stages at the child's rate of development, and mostly based on his automatic reflexes. The process had been conscious enough for the child to progress and to be able to master a repertoire of several pieces. But the children were now fifteen years old and had reached a ceiling beyond which they could not progress any more, although they could go on learning new pieces. Nevertheless the achievement gave them an emotional outlet and a social status among other children that they could not have gained in any other way.

The retarded child who has absorbed music in the right way during his school years may go on enjoying it later on. Girls are more bent on singing and boys on instrumental playing. The following description is typical of a music session in a boys' youth club:

In our music making clubs (for retarded boys) we have used drums with wire brushes, the tea-chest bass, bones, spoons, and guitars to provide the rhythm for tunes played on combs and paper, or sung. One or two boys have shown great interest in guitars and they could quite well learn the tonic, dominant and sub-dominant chords in the common keys, or use an instrument with a chording attachment.[19]

Anyone attending a musical session with backward children cannot help being struck by the unusual liveliness and happiness shown on their faces and by their purposeful behaviour. The backward boy was quite conscious of his feelings who stated what he liked best at school: 'I like Fridays because of 'ymns and singing—it jollies you up, like.'[20]

LISTENING TO MUSIC

But the experience of music is indivisible, and the child who is taught to sing, or to play an instrument, should also be trained to listen to music. He may as a listener experience deeper emotions than in making music himself and communicate with a world of expressive sounds that he cannot produce with his limited means. The following summaries of some of my experiments in this field describe one method through which a retarded child can become a good listener and experience great joys in the process.

[19] Tansley and Gulliford, op. cit., p. 185.
[20] E. A. Taylor, *Experiments with a Backward Class* (1952).

6

THE MENTALLY SUBNORMAL CHILD

LISTENING TO MUSIC

THE VALUE OF LIVE PERFORMANCE

The success of musical activities for the mentally retarded child depends primarily on his auditory perception and his power of attention. It is these two faculties that allow the interpretation of sound, and it is through their development that the experience of music can be really beneficial to the handicapped child.

I have made a special study of how the ability of handicapped children to listen to music can be developed. I have tested this ability at all levels and have studied various methods and techniques. Training subnormal children is bound to be a very slow and gradual process. The child has first to be emotionally and intellectually motivated in order to sustain his attention long enough to hear and to remember. The best method I have found is one that appeals to the child in a number of ways, namely a live performance of music.

The following pages are a summary of many experiments which I have made in E.S.N. schools and in training centres for mentally handicapped children, on children suffering from different types and degrees of mental retardation. The techniques were based on the natural emotional response of children to music and consisted in weekly live performances of music given in the classroom to separate age groups of ten to fifteen children. Although basically similar the programmes were strictly adapted to the degree of retardation of the children. Everywhere the work was planned in order to elicit from each child an emotional response and to provoke an awareness related to his condition.

The music sessions aimed at developing the children's auditory, visual, and tactile perception. They were prompted to take an active mental and sometimes physical participation in the proceedings, and were helped to express themselves spontaneously and naturally. This all-round stimulation aimed at increasing their power of observation and retention.

The emotional and psychological impact of the experience awoke in most children a desire for self-expression which could be exploited to full advantage at the time, or in the classroom later on. With the E.S.N. child it was transferred to school subjects such as written and oral work, art, craft, and others. Most of the music was related to the child's life in order to appeal to his emotions and to provoke his imagination. In the E.S.N. schools the work was based round the children's reading books, and all other subjects to which music could be related. The children's curiosity and interest were constantly kept alive, and we tried to widen their field of general knowledge.

With the severely subnormal child, whose responses were much more primitive and inarticulate, my aim was directed at another level. We tried to reach the child's consciousness; to establish communication with him; to socialize him; to provoke in him reactions of curiosity and interest; to awake his desire to move, or to imitate, or to participate, or to verbalize. I tried to develop in him some power of attention and observation.

It was interesting to note that the curve of improvement which took place between the point of departure and the ceiling reached was very similar and of the same kind in E.S.N. and the severely subnormal children. I started at the the child's own level which was pretty low in the training centres and sometimes surprisingly high in E.S.N. schools.

The detailed reports made by the heads and the staff at both places were quite similar and interesting to compare, since the same kinds of reaction and development had been observed.

THE AUTHOR'S EXPERIENCES

The weekly music sessions varied from fifteen to thirty minutes. About two-thirds of the time was devoted to the actual music performance. The remainder consisted of the presentation of the 'cello and of its components; verbal comments adapted to the level of the children, and the handling of various objects. The session ended with an experience offered to each of the children to come forward, hold the bow, and move it across the strings in order to produce a tone himself. This was not only a treat for the children, but a psychological test, the results of which sometimes were revealing to the child's teacher. The experience also showed a gradual development in general self-control and confidence, since the child who came forward voluntarily had to stand alone in front of the group and produce a sound on the 'cello. During the proceedings the other children usually were orderly and attentive: they wanted to hear what kind of tone the others would produce. There was great merriment without malice when it sounded unusual. The movement the children tried to make showed that they had carefully watched the movements of the performer. Most of them waited eagerly for the experience that seemed to crystallize the impact and certainly helped to stamp in the effect of the music session.

Whenever possible I added tactile perception to auditory and visual perception in order to provoke on all sides, and to increase, the child's awareness. The handling of some objects such as the mute, the resin, strings, pegs, and others during and after the concert added greatly to the children's interest and gave reality to the experience. It also provided a useful change between two pieces of music if the listening power of the children showed signs of weakening. Although unfamiliar, the objects passed round were linked to things well known to the children (some were made of wood, or came from an animal, or looked like a comb or a nail). The children observed them carefully and sometimes drew them accurately from memory.

During the sessions I used means that could be repeated again and again so that familiarity became knowledge, increased the enjoyment, and helped towards the development of sense perception. I tried each time to enlarge the area of the purely musical experience. As the children's span of attention increased I was able to lengthen each of the musical items and add others to the programme. The conscious span of attention of the severely subnormal children was sometimes at the beginning not longer than twenty seconds, but later on they were able to listen attentively to pieces lasting more than two minutes. The same relative improvement was observed in the E.S.N. children with whom I could generally start right away with longer items of one to two minutes.

At the beginning of each session, and throughout a series, the opening of the 'cello case was watched intensely by all the children and created an atmosphere of expectation. Once this feeling had been aroused it was possible to provoke the children's curiosity and to awaken their interest. The main task was to sustain it long enough. Throughout the session the appeal made alternatively to the children's imagination and their sense of realism helped to renew and to sustain their attention. The staff in the E.S.N. schools noticed that 'the children's interest was aroused at once, and that there was much reaction and interest even in the dullest pupils who otherwise were always inattentive and uninterested'. In their various reports the staff expressed the opinion that 'the music sessions were certainly a help towards the general development of mental concentration and power of observation'.

The programme included tunes that had structure and made a simple melodic and rhythmical appeal to the child. Sometimes it was only a fragment of a piece, but it was always constructed, had a beginning, a middle, and an end. I also made the children hear various effects of tone, intensity, rhythm, and speed as produced on the 'cello. They responded well to these experiences. For instance, many of them found very dramatic a long crescendo and diminuendo on one sustained note; they were impressed by the use of the mute and loved the tone it produces; they followed attentively the sound of two simultaneous parts imitating the bagpipes, played on two strings, and they tried to follow the movement of the bow on the strings. This helped them to perceive whether one or two notes were played together. This approach through a single experience of sound was very effective. The children often clapped spontaneously after hearing a dissociated effect of this type, a response that showed emotional satisfaction.

They found exciting any change of tone colour. The E.S.N. children were interested in auditory games; for instance, in closing their eyes and guessing whether a sound had been plucked or played with the bow, or had been loud or soft, or high or low. These techniques and many others were part of the exploration of sound primarily helped by the sight of the instrument.

Movement is an emotion to any child, and I tried to relate music to that feeling. Notes that can run, march, hop, bounce, skip, stop, or start are produced by a visible bow movement corresponding to the effect. It was observed that the children became more and more aware of the rhythmical character of some pieces. After a few weeks the E.S.N. children did not confuse any more the dancing movement of a gavotte or a minuet with a march or running steps, even in pieces they were hearing for the first time.

As their perception and awareness increased, the children reacted better and better to the mood of the music. They could even use quite accurate words to express the character of certain pieces, such as: happy, clumsy, excited, funny, light, serious, heavy, quiet, near and far, and so on. A few children were able to qualify it with a sentence. I did not try to get such accurate verbal reactions from the severely subnormal children. But even so a number of them remembered the titles of the pieces, expressed some preference and asked for them. They remembered the names of certain objects passed round to handle. Their teachers noticed how much they verbalized during and after the sessions.

At a different degree this slow but progressive process enabled the children in the schools and in the centres to acquire a certain amount of auditory and musical discrimination. Their memory of sounds and their memory of words and facts connected with them gradually increased. This improvement was tested each week, not on their immediate retention but on a longer term memory. With the E.S.N. children it was done with music which had not been played on that day, but one or several weeks before. After a few sessions some of the E.S.N. children were able to state verbally and from memory how a certain piece started or ended: for instance, with a loud plucked note or with a long, soft note; or how many times a certain musical effect such as the cuckoo song was repeated in the piece; or when the mute had to be put on and why; or what happened during a piece, not necessarily a story; and so on. The children's enjoyment grew in relation to their awareness and acquired knowledge, and so did their attention.

The emotional and mental stimulus provoked by the music showed in other ways than in the improvement of specific memory. It helped the children to express themselves in words, writing, drawing and painting, and also in movements to the music. In the E.S.N. schools the staff noticed that 'material and ideas provided by the music sessions were valuable especially in oral work; the children were beginning to express themselves better in words'. Nevertheless I noticed that in some E.S.N. schools most of the young children could not pronounce any word clearly and many of them were unable to find their words. When asked to choose a piece they made a single gesture such as a rotary movement of the hand to indicate that they wanted the 'Bicycle Ride'. When they wished to play on two strings a few did not speak, they just extended two fingers. Very few senior children were able to tell a full story, although they knew the right sequence of events. But even in the low grade children I noticed an improvement in verbalization probably due in part to the building up of self-confidence.

Since many children were not able to find an outlet in spoken or written words, we made them express themselves as well and spontaneously through movements to music. But we wanted movement to help and not disturb their active and conscious process of listening. The movements through which they were prompted to express themselves were solely movements of hands and arms, and facial expression. The children did not leave their seats and kept on listening. Little by little they learned how to control these movements and to avoid any that could make a noise. Many pieces in the programme did not call for movement, and the children could learn the enjoyment of listening when they were physically relaxed.

In the 'Bicycle Ride' they imitated the wheels with only a rotary movement of the hands since they were supposed to go down the hill free-wheeling and to keep their feet still; during the 'Soldier's March' their arms moved stiffly like a wooden toy's; they made light movements of the fingers to imitate the 'Doll's Dance'; some started spontaneously blowing an imaginary pipe during the 'Snake Charmer'; in the 'Cradle Song' they rocked the baby to sleep or went to sleep themselves; during the 'Butterfly' all hands were up fluttering in the air. These movements and many others helped them to remember the music. The movements were at first clumsy and uncontrolled; they improved gradually and fitted better with the music. I often kept them waiting in silence and prepared to move, and they enjoyed the sudden start. In the end they achieved a complex performance which combined movement with auditory and visual perception.[1]

The piece was in three parts: first the Doll's Dance, then the Toy Soldier's March, then the Doll's Dance again. The March was in pizzicati, which meant a perceptible change in the tone and the instrumental technique. Before we started, the children pretended to wind up the toy soldier and held the key tightly during the Doll's Dance. When they heard the March they immediately released the key and started moving their arms with the rhythm. They stopped at the return of the Doll's Dance. I used with much success their sense of controlled expectation, that can be developed so easily through music.

Something similar happened spontaneously in a training centre. The children expressed their pleasure in clapping at the end of the pieces they liked; it was a sign of conscious appreciation as well as a physical outlet. Some of the children from the beginning of a favourite piece got their hands up ready for the clapping movement and kept them immobile until the very end of the piece. Then, and then only, they let go with enthusiasm. This became a sign of special appreciation that had not been prompted.

---

[1] Some of these titles are mine. I often played only one significant passage out of a piece, and the title was then related to the effect it made on the children. It sometimes happened that the title was suggested by the children t hemselves.

I tried everywhere to create first a general atmosphere of happiness, humour, and confidence, which is essential with the E.S.N. and the severely subnormal child. I noticed that many of the young E.S.N. children tried to sit as near the 'cello as possible and seemed to be in a state of happy expectation. Many times when they heard the musicians arrive at the front door they started to clap spontaneously and loudly. The severely subnormal expressed in the same way their pleasurable expectation. At some of the training centres when the children filed into the classroom and noticed the 'cello case standing in a corner they expressed their satisfaction by clapping, rubbing their hands together, groaning, smiling, and exclaiming. In fact, many of the lower type were much more aware of the 'cello than of the musicians, whom they sometimes did not even recognize.

In E.S.N. schools and training centres alike, I worked with two main groups, the hyperactive and uncontrolled, and the apathetic and unresponsive type. These characteristics were not related to age or sex, and I noticed them in boys and girls, and in young children and adolescents.

In the hyperactive, volatile groups the children were uncontrolled and expressed their emotions forcibly and antisocially. I never imposed discipline or introduced moral issues of behaviour which would have destroyed the atmosphere of free happiness we were aiming at. But improvement in self-control set in gradually by itself. Little by little the children discovered that uncontrolled behaviour and noise prevented them from enjoying the music. Unless the children were emotionally disturbed, I made them practise self-control by playing in succession extremely contrasting pieces. They were given an opportunity to let off steam in an exciting piece, and then to calm down immediately. For instance, the first time they heard a reel they became so excited that they almost stopped listening. But when they heard, immediately after, one of their soft favourite pieces, they quietened down at once. If there was some stamping of feet during a march, the Swan came as an immediate sedative, great silence fell throughout the piece, and was followed by loud clapping at the end.

The staff noticed many instances of improvement in the behaviour of difficult children, such as Peter, who was always changing his place and occupation and who became able to sit calmly during the whole concert without anything to amuse him and to enjoy the music. Or John, who was always making disturbing noises and could not keep still. Gradually he took an interest in the music and was able to listen well. One day he even asked me if I could play a tractor. I satisfied him in telling him that the Elephant was driving a tractor in the music.

The groups of withdrawn and lethargic children presented me with other kinds of difficulties. The problem was not in channelling an uncontrolled activity, but in awakening an interest. They were not ready to move with the music, but they sang with obvious pleasure with the 'cello which gave them support and confidence. Their reactions to the music were brief, such as smiles, or a sudden satisfied silence which was not a sign of apathy. I had to watch for individual reactions since many of the children were more withdrawn than apathetic. Many observations were taken on individual cases which were of particular interest to the teachers. For instance, Mark, an emotionally disturbed boy whom the teacher considered as intelligent. He was a child who had never opened up before strangers. But 'in the first concert he was the first one to go out and play a note. In the classroom he had never given the appearance to be listening to stories, had always sat with a blank look on his face and when asked a question could only repeat the question. Yet in the concerts his face showed that he was listening. When the class was asked what piece they would like to hear he asked for the Stream which he had heard only once before and which no one else seemed to remember.'

I also found some children who were deeply disturbed and withdrawn. Mary, in an E.S.N. school, was a mongoloid girl who could not write, or read, or draw. She sat during five sessions, obstinately shut up in herself as she did everywhere. But I noticed that she gradually looked more lively, less indifferent, and seemed to follow the music. Nevertheless she was the only one in the group who did not come forward at the end to play a note on the 'cello. But at the end of a later session, when the other children had come forward, I noticed that tears were rolling down her cheeks. When she looked calmer, I went up to her and took her by the hand. She followed with docility, took the bow in her hand and played. I noticed how attentive she was, how well she followed the bow movement, and how deeply satisfied she looked. From that day she became part of the group and displayed much liveliness.

Innate apathy was difficult to overcome, but I used all possible means to stir up the children. First I tried to provoke physical responses to rhythm that are compulsive reactions, and to awake their curiosity, that even a passive child finds difficult to resist. These two basic physical and emotional responses helped me to build up a programme aiming at sustaining and developing their reactions. I gave special importance to the timing and to the place of each item on the programme. I could build nothing constructive unless the child was impressed at the right time, deeply and long enough to remember the experience.

I noticed in all children that their immediate reaction to a piece did not always indicate how much they would remember of it. I came to the conclusion that however effective it seemed to be at the time, if the piece was too long or too fast they kept very little memory of it. For example, a brilliant and fast Tarantella lasting five minutes played in an E.S.N. school was followed by tremendous applause, but no child remembered it the following week, although they remembered a number of other pieces played on that day. Therefore, although some pieces were given for the sake of immediate pleasure that left no conscious trace, the purpose of most items was constructive. It aimed at feeding the child's mind with lasting experiences. This could be achieved even in the training centres where many children recognized the tunes they had heard and where many of them made requests for their favourite pieces to be played.

The musical emotion and the knowledge which the children absorbed were in some cases transferred to other creative activities. It was done through team work between the teachers and the musicians. The stimulus of the music session could give an added emotional meaning to vocabulary, to the concept of numbers, to reading or writing, to Art, History, Geography, or Nature. Some pieces of music were related to the children's reading books; the notes in the music were units that could be counted in figures. Many children expressed their feelings about the music in writing, painting, or craft. Much of the work that had been motivated by music was considered to be somewhat above their ordinary standard.

I observed the same basic reactions in the E.S.N. adolescent as in the younger children, but I had to take a different approach with the older boys and girls. The discrepancy between their physical, their mental, and their emotional development was more obvious than in the younger children and I had to offer them a seemingly more adult experience that they could interpret at their own level. They often felt a desire to participate but in different ways. Adolescent boys did not want to sing with the 'cello, but the girls did. Most of the boys were happy to click their fingers and to imitate the castanets, or tap the rhythm during Spanish dances. These techniques and others were musically more advanced since they had to fit in with the music in an orderly way.

Except in the case of groups of very low subnormals, most of the older retarded children I met had already acquired a sense of social behaviour and many of them were socially integrated. This sometimes prevented them from responding in the raw, primitive way that I could observe in younger children. Many of the E.S.N. adolescent girls were self-conscious and afraid of giving themselves away. The adolescent boys were more candid; often they would differ openly in their preference for certain pieces of music. But under that surface I discovered in many of them an unconscious, and often unfulfilled need, for experiences at a deeper emotional level. They did not want only the physically exciting type of music that is supposed to 'go down' well with them. It was natural for the girls to like music with a sentimental appeal, but the boys as well could be touched by beauty at a deep level. Music such as the 'Air' by Bach, 'Lullaby' by Brahms, the 'Hindoo Song', the 'Habanera' by Ravel, traditional melodies, and many others satisfied in them an unspoken need.

I tried to give these youngsters an experience that was not self-contained and to train them sufficiently to make them want to hear more music, perhaps in real concerts outside the school. I often referred to some of the pieces as being in the repertoire of famous performers. When the children heard the piece in broadcast or television performances they were thrilled and showed surprising discrimination in their comments. Other children started to make scrapbooks on themes related to the music sessions. Some of them expressed a wish to learn a musical instrument in order to join a club. One of the E.S.N. teachers took her class to the Public Library and showed them easy books on music and musicians. In these and many other ways music could be related to life outside school. It could then take another significance than if it had been restricted to the children's own limited achievement. I tried to give them contact with music itself at a high standard. Without undue optimism or illusions I tried to open a world of aesthetic and emotional joys to many of these children who, because of their poverty of mind, might never find another way towards the finest things in life.

7

THE MALADJUSTED CHILD

MALADJUSTMENT is the inability to form satisfactory relationships with oneself, with people and with one's environment. It is a disorder of deviant personality which has many causes and takes many forms.

Maladjustment may be caused by some inborn defect of personality affecting the child's relations with his environment, or by some emotional stress for which the child was unprepared, too sensitive or too young at the time. This kind of maladjustment is quite different from the maladjustment due to a physical disability that produces emotional difficulties of adjustment and integration. In the latter case the treatment consists of making the child accept his disability and come to terms with it, of teaching him to live with it, and offering him creative substitutes and compensations that can develop him to the full of his potentials. We should consider this form of indirect maladjustment as the result and not the cause of a disorder.

When the disturbance is purely emotional and not due to other causes we do not try to make the child accept his disorder and live with it. We try to eliminate the disorder and to help the child to grow in harmony with his environment. In this chapter I propose to discuss how music can help the child to develop satisfactory relationships at different levels of consciousness.

Whatever the direct cause, the maladjusted child has been and is emotionally frustrated; he rejects or resists a world with which he cannot integrate; he fights against anything that is orderly and organized. 'A constant feature of maladjustment is a tendency to rebel against authority.'[1] This rebellious attitude makes the child destructive of his own inner peace, and when he associates it is usually for destructive or disruptive ends. He may either refuse to grow up and then take refuge

[1] J. D. Kershaw, *Handicapped Children* (1961), p. 174.

in a regressed and negative attitude, or he may try to assert himself in telling lies, stealing, running away from home or in forming undesirable associations.

We can observe many different kinds of behaviour in a class of maladjusted children. Some of them exteriorize their disorder in an uncontrolled way, are hyperactive, quarrelsome, noisy, and undisciplined. Some suffer from tantrums or tempers; others withdraw: they are shy, suspicious, obstinate, and sulky. Whatever his symptoms, the maladjusted child lives in a chaotic world of emotions which prevent him from relating and integrating. He may miss the opportunities to be educated and to develop. Moreover, many causes of maladjustment due to bad environment, such as unsatisfactory family relations, are difficult to remove or even to improve, and the child attending a day school often finds himself caught in a vicious circle of conflicting influences.

HOW MALADJUSTED CHILDREN CAN BENEFIT FROM MUSIC

The maladjusted child has two principal needs—one for satisfying human relationship, the other for satisfying emotional experiences that come from sources other than personal contacts and can help to liberate him. Music may help to answer these two needs because it provokes both human contact and contact with an emotional world which is impersonal. Furthermore, the child may be able to accept himself and others through musical activities, and also find in music great emotional release and happiness.

Since the maladjusted child has difficulty in forming satisfactory relationships, there is no other child with whom the teacher-child relationship plays a bigger part towards success or failure. The teacher's personality, his attitudes, his likes and dislikes, or his moods, however controlled, have a deep influence on the emotionally disturbed child. This child is emotionally vulnerable in spite of the barriers he erects between himself and the world. A change of teacher may upset him in a disastrous way and provoke increased revolt or withdrawal. The teacher should be to this child a stable individual whose behaviour and attitudes are constant and predictable, and give him a sense of security. He should offer the child the love and understanding that are needed, but not be possessive or emotional. The teacher who is proficient in some creative pursuit, such as music or art, that appeals to the child, may share many pleasant experiences with him, and thus build up a satisfactory relationship. With music this can happen best if the teacher can play to the children who listen. This relationship helps to develop mutual respect. The teacher should use his imagination to make music significant. Music should not be just 'fun' or something that 'goes down well'. Those are trite terms, too often used, and which belittle the true value of music to handicapped children.

The music teacher can also help the child to establish good relationship with the music itself—a relationship that should be non-verbal and non-threatening. Nevertheless music contains elements that create fear, or undesirable tension or hypnosis, or provoke physiopsychological reflexes that a maladjusted child cannot control. High pitched notes, sudden contrasts can be disturbing because they are tense and unexpected. High speed or strong percussive rhythms may get a whole group of disturbed children out of control because of their compulsive effect. Also what is called 'soothing' music may not always make a good effect on the child when he is in need of more lively experiences, or when he feels so agitated and tense that softness cannot reach him.

On the whole the maladjusted child wants to hear music that gives him a sense of lively security in the world of sound, a security that does not necessarily come from a feeling of relaxation. At a deeper level the child may get an unconscious sense of security from the fact that what he hears is his own —and that no one can interfere with or disturb his personal interpretation of the music. He is free, but within bounds.

Music may help to relieve the maladjusted child from his egocentric obsession. It can reveal and open to him a world in which his emotions are projected in a satisfactory way and do not create conflicts. It is difficult to choose suitable music to play to maladjusted children. Some of it lies outside the ordinary school repertoire because it should be selected for psychological as well as for musical purposes.

THERAPY

Music makes a deep effect on the maladjusted child because sounds penetrate into the subconscious and cannot be resisted. Here we are entering a field in which music is allied to psychotherapy. Although it has been stated that 'all special education is therapeutic'[2] the music teacher must be specially trained and equipped before he may rightly be called a music therapist and undertake the kind of work we now propose to discuss.

It is often thought that creative art including music is based on material which has arisen from the unconscious mind of the artist. Music in turn may stimulate the unconscious mind of the child. I have observed that certain musical experiences help to bring up to the surface deep-seated matter of which the child becomes conscious and with which he may then be able to deal provided that he gets the necessary help. This process is not an escape into fantasy, but a return to reality and may bring inexpressible relief to a tormented child. Among many instances, I could quote the following case of a very disturbed boy of ten called Martin. He lived in a home for maladjusted children in which the children voluntarily attended recorded performances of music. One evening, before bedtime, the Vaughan Williams *Sinfonia Antartica* was played. During the session some children went to sleep:

Whether Martin did actually sleep during the session, I am not sure. But certainly he became very relaxed as he lay curled up in an armchair with his eyes closed, and he did not appear to be awake when, at the end, he was carried upstairs and placed in his bed.

The next day, Martin came up to me: 'Skipper', he said, 'that music we had last night . . . it made me think of my Dad . . . and I dreamt about him all night too. . . .' Then he sobbed and said: 'I shall be eighteen before I see my Dad again . . . before my Dad comes out of prison. . . .'

. . . Music gave him release, which enabled him to talk more freely to me, and to our consultant psychiatrist, about his Dad in prison, and about his unhappy and frightening feelings—and about his

[2] Conference of Workers of Maladjusted Children, Nottingham, 1962.

resentful feelings, too. Early in life he had been unbalanced by causes[3] beyond his understanding. No wonder he was backward and un- happy, disturbed and disturbing. No wonder he was at loggerheads with himself, and causing storms to upset and to unbalance others.

Music is often associated with well-known projective tech- niques used with the disturbed child. In psychodrama, or just in 'acting out' his trouble, the maladjusted child can find relief and be liberated from unconscious emotions and desires against which he may be fighting. In a group of disturbed children to whom I was playing a cradle song a very small and inarticulate boy suddenly tried to strangle and then throw on the floor the imaginary baby he was rocking in his arms. He then looked round slyly to see if anyone had noticed him. It was the first time that he had shown these hidden feelings.

When the child is in need of acting a long and painful story buried in the subconscious, the sound of music which is immaterial, elusive, and continuous can help to go through to the end. In that case the musician should improvise music that supports the child's action through continuity and rhythm; follow his movements in the background, with music of the right mood and not impose or suggest anything through music or speech. The child left alone then may go through the whole sequence, as did a very sick little girl in a centre for severely maladjusted children. The teacher improvised music which gave the child some incentive to move about. The little girl went round and round, imagining herself in a dark wood in the moonlight, looking for something, she did not know what. She searched under the fallen leaves, found a baby doll, and started eating it. It is doubtful that she would have gone through the whole experience without the help of the music.[4]

At the superego level a child in revolt and full of ugly feelings may experience sublimation through music, and feel great relief in the contact with something good and beautiful. This is in her own words what happened to a girl of fourteen in a

[3] Frank E. Knight, 'Music Therapy with Maladjusted Children', paper read at London Conference of the Society for Music Therapy and Remedial Music, 1960.

[4] Quoted by Miss Ruth Armitage, Meeting of the Society for Music Therapy and Remedial Music, March 1960.

home for badly disturbed children. She was intelligent and thought of herself as 'a horrible and nasty girl not worth bothering about'. She wrote the following lines after attending a concert in which she was enthralled and behaved exceptionally well:

After the concert when I went to bed, the sweet lovely tunes kept on repeating in my ears. What a lovely day full of *goodness* and *beauty* it has been.

And she underlined the two significant words. Aaron Copland expresses the same feelings when he says that great music 'awakens in us reactions of a spiritual order that are already in us, only waiting to be aroused'.[5] This disturbed girl had a terribly low and pessimistic opinion of herself. The unexpected feelings of beauty and goodness she experienced may have helped her to revaluate herself and given her hope.

Another time I was invited to play to three groups of boys in a psychiatric centre for delinquents. There were twenty boys in each group, from fourteen to eighteen years old, intelligent, very disturbed, aggressive, and known for their antisocial behaviour. Many of them were known to the police. They were willing to associate freely only towards destructive ends.

Twenty in each group was the maximum number possible, and even then there was a danger of finding in the group leaders who would try to disrupt. The staff was not too optimistic.

I did not ask for any discipline—only interest, which was intense from the beginning—during an experience which was to the boys totally new and unexpected. I treated them as any other intelligent and sensitive audience whom I respect and with whom I share my pleasure in music. Each face in this audience was marked with deep trouble and looked as if nothing good or happy could ever happen. But their interest was immediately aroused. The boys relaxed when they found an experience that could be stimulating without tension, and in a world in which it was easy not to revolt. The programme was made to appeal to their intelligence, their imagination,

[5] *Music and Imagination*, p. 26.

and enabled them to display some knowledge. I was able to handle them with a sense of humour—something quite rare with boys who are suspicious and ready to take offence. From beginning to end each of the groups showed attention, interest, and enthusiasm.

A few days after the performance a number of the boys asked the psychiatrist in charge if they could form a music club in the home. This very unexpected request was an added proof that the musical experience had answered an emotional need and might help them towards creative and constructive activities.

HARMFUL EFFECTS OF MUSIC

Those few examples among many show how a disturbed child can benefit from music, when it is used at the proper place and in the right way. But there are also many cases where music can produce in the child undesirable and even harmful effects. This is true of children who want to escape from the outer world of reality around them, a world that has frustrated them and which makes on them demands they are not willing to answer. To these children all means of escape are welcome, whether playing truant from school or absconding or creating in their mind a world of dream and fancy.

We have already described how the emotionally disturbed child can be hypnotized by certain kinds of music, especially music containing monotonous and repetitive rhythms. The 'Bolero' by Ravel is a typical example, the 'Valse Triste' by Sibelius, or any piece based on African rhythms.

MAKING MUSIC

The maladjusted child needs satisfying relationship with reality through an experience that is mentally, physically, and emotionally secure. He can find this experience in making music.

In the preceding pages we have discussed the effect of music on the subconscious, as a relief from emotional urges that are deep-seated. But the child can also experience emotional relief when he makes music himself. He can, like all other children, find in music a means of social integration, of intellectual and emotional development.

Making music is a conscious experience in which the whole child is in action, through which he can relate and identify. The child who makes music has to make purposeful and directed physical movements. The unity of purpose and the reality of this activity may help him to relax emotionally. Then he should set free his imagination, which is still kept within reasonable bounds by the very musical rules he should follow. A maladjusted child who relaxes and can at the same time be engaged in some creative activity should function at his best.

Music in the classroom includes many activities, and I shall now discuss schoolroom techniques, including the use of the voice, the choice of instruments and music, and the handling of the music group.

THE TEACHER'S VOICE AND HIS MUSICAL SKILL

The maladjusted child is particularly sensitive to the nature and the quality of the sounds that reach him, and this does not apply to music alone. The teacher may not be aware that the quality of his own speaking voice can affect the maladjusted child. I have observed that a naturally high-pitched voice—or a voice pitched too high in order to sound jolly—may make an adverse effect on the tense child; on the other hand, a medium or low-pitched voice, firm and well articulated, is a definite asset to the teacher of maladjusted children because its timbre gives a feeling of confidence and helps communication, whatever the voice says.

If the speaking voice of the teacher expresses much of his personality, so does his playing music on any instrument, or his singing. If he makes music to the children, his attitude towards his own playing and the music is more important than the standard of his performance—provided that it is a live and convincing one which the children will feel is good. Disturbed children often have a devastating insight into people and are quick to detect any lack of confidence, complacency, or condescension—all attitudes that can destroy their trust and their pleasure and lead to bad behaviour.

Many music teachers are proficient on one instrument which they use in the classroom. We have already (pp. 78 ff.) discussed the value of various musical instruments that handicapped children can learn to play themselves. But when the instrument is played by the teacher other factors should be considered, for the instrument then becomes a vital means of communication between the teacher and the child.

The piano is a useful and maybe an indispensable instrument in any schoolroom for general use. But the opinion of experienced music teachers of handicapped children is that the piano is far from ideal to use as a means of communication with a group of maladjusted children who are difficult to reach, difficult to control, and to integrate—although it is excellent for individual work with some psychotic or autistic children (see pp. 110 ff.). When working with a group the teacher at the piano has to turn his back to the room and therefore to most of the children, except those who can stand or sit at his side. He cannot easily see or feel what the group is doing or forecast what they are going to do. Moreover, he has to stay where he is, and even if he takes notice of the children to them he usually seems much concerned with the keyboard which is a vast expanse of space. The tone of the piano also is not quite suitable, being too percussive and carrying an element of compulsion that is often undesirable with maladjusted children.

Some young maladjusted children are jealous of the piano that seems to take too much of the teacher's attention. Others are afraid of it, like the little girl who had a pathological fear of its big white and black teeth.[6]

A portable instrument such as the flute or the recorder, the guitar or the auto-harp, can be carried round and enable the teacher to move in the room. He is free to play to and to contact any individual child, or to form a small group either standing or sitting around him. He can then follow or direct any physical activity associated with the music. A portable

[6] Frank E. Knight, 'Music Therapy with Maladjusted Children', Conference of the Society for Music Therapy and Remedial Music, London, 1960.

instrument can be shown round and manipulated by the children; this greatly helps to centre their interest on the instrument itself, provoke some respect for it, and possibly motivate the child who could learn to play. In all this work the music teacher is only a secondary figure. The children often call me 'the music lady' or 'Mrs. Cello' because what seems to matter is the music and the instrument, and as a person I do try to keep in the background.

The flute is one of the best instruments to provoke communication with a group of maladjusted children in the classroom, for both psychological and musical reasons. Its tone is beautiful, persuasive but not compulsive. It possesses 'a certain objective lyricism, a kind of ethereal fluidity'.[7] It sounds immaterial and effortless when well produced. Moreover, the flute has a wide range of expression, can be soothing or very lively, and rhythmical without being percussive. For that reason it cannot produce strong physical reflexes which are difficult to control, and it has a good varied repertoire of music of all kinds.

The guitar and some other instruments on which the strings are plucked produces a more stimulating effect and may provoke the attention of the withdrawn child who lives in his own world. The guitar is musically more versatile than the flute because it can be used for accompaniment as well as for solo work. Owing to its traditional and rhythmical character the guitar has a splendid repertoire of folk music and contemporary dances of many countries which makes a direct appeal to any child. The guitar is also associated in the child's mind with very desirable adolescent or adult music-making groups, either amateur or professional.

THE MUSIC-MAKING GROUP

Music-making enables the disturbed child to release pent-up emotions with a minimum of discipline. This aspect has been treated in the preceding chapters and is particularly important with children whose behaviour and attitudes are basically antisocial and who associate too easily towards undesirable ends.

[7] Aaron Copland, *Music and Imagination*, p. 39.

We find in the same group of maladjusted children two opposite types which are difficult to integrate in an activity group: the over-active and uncontrolled type whose behaviour should be stabilized, and the inhibited anxious conformist whose initiative should be stimulated. Both types have in common their inability to keep attentive, not from intellectual but from emotional causes. They may feel deeply for a short time, but they cannot keep for long in the same mood and often dart from one experience to another.

In the music-making group the teacher should let the music itself make its demands on the child. Keeping good time and rhythm, following the dynamics, playing the right note, caring for intonation are basic musical rules that the teacher himself has to obey. Ideally the child who is willing to follow these rules should behave well, provided that the effort does not outwear his feeble power of attention. He can be shown that his own enjoyment of music depends on tolerable behaviour. If he disturbs it he should be taken out of the group, never as a punishment, but for the simple reason that if he does not enjoy making music or listening to it he need not be there.

The child who suffers from emotional disorder may express himself individually in a disorderly way when he makes music and experience great emotional release in the process. But, like the immature child, he is not yet ready to join a group. The music teacher should let him be as free as possible to make music by himself, and not with others, on a suitable instrument. Little by little the teacher may help him individually to curb his aggressive treatment of the instrument, or to give up his bad vocal manners. If this is not at all possible, then there is no reason why the child should not release his aggressiveness or exercise his bad vocal habits on other things than on what should be 'music'.

MATERIAL FOR GROUP WORK

At the beginning the work with a music group of mal-adjusted children is very experimental and tentative. The music teacher should not attempt to plan musical activities on an organized basis. He would be frustrated at once. He has first to offer his group a very varied programme, including all kinds of musical activities, or activities related to music: singing, dancing, playing, listening, story-telling, miming, and so on. Each of these activities should be kept as short as possible, and the teacher should have at his immediate disposal an infinite means of action, music, instruments, records, and also spontaneous ideas, through which he can follow as closely as possible the changing mood of the group. These activities will elicit many responses from the children, favourable or adverse, that have to be observed and interpreted psychologically and musically. The music teacher should be able to detect where a musical development may take place and of which kind— which relationship can grow within the group that could be used in music. He can also at an early stage assess the musical sensibility of each of the children and his emotional or physical response to music (see pp. 9–10).

It is often difficult to choose the right kind of music to use with such a disparate group of children who express their emotional needs in such different ways. Even regressed, their feelings can be much more violent than those of other handicapped children, and the music they want is not of the tame kind. The music session should include music that relaxes the mood and music that stimulates the imagination. It should be of a kind that gives a sense of security, through even speed and rhythm and an easy-flowing melody in which the expected happens. It need not be hackneyed. Much imaginative music exists that is easy for the child to play in any type of school ensemble—beautiful to listen to and enjoy.

In singing or choral work with maladjusted children, songs should be chosen for the suitability of the text. With disturbed children one should take care to avoid disturbing or undesirable associations of words or situations that may upset the child or antagonize him. This happened with a maladjusted crippled little girl, who reacted violently to a song 'thanking God for His Blessings' and cried 'What should I be grateful for?'; or a motherless neglected child hearing a song about mother's tender love.

The best songs for groups of maladjusted children should

relate to a world of concrete situations and actions that are enjoyable, possibly with a sense of humour; songs that give lively, exciting but orderly impressions of movement and life; others that transform ordinary daily things and make them imaginative, harmonious, or beautiful; others that are realistic and appeal to the sense of realism in the child—and others that are lyrical and appeal to his imagination.

Throughout his troubled childhood and adolescence, the emotionally disturbed child can find in music much to help him and to relieve him. It may help him to realize himself and give him an emotional outlet of exceptional value.

8

THE AUTISTIC PSYCHOTIC CHILD

INFANTILE autism is a grave disorder of communication now recognized as a psychotic state distinct from severe subnormality. Its causes are still unknown in spite of recent research at international level. It can be diagnosed from its most severe form to what is called 'autistic tendencies' which may be observed in other handicapped children such as the maladjusted or the severely subnormal who are not psychotic. But as the autistic child is unable to communicate and cannot be reached the causes or extent of his disorder are difficult to diagnose or to treat. Whatever form they take, autistic symptoms affect the whole learning process and create deep obstacles to the development of human relationships. We are faced with the child's mental, emotional, and social problems due to his pathological behaviour. The symptoms of autism include a morbid concentration upon self, an inability to communicate normally, ritualistic obsessive behaviour. The child exhibits temper tantrums, anxiety, incomprehensible fears or panic. He suffers from perceptual anomalies and abnormal cognitive processes. He lacks warmth, is aloof and cold, either withdrawn or hyperactive. He seems to live in a closed world, which may be a refuge or a prison.

Such an unfortunate inward-turned child presents an acute challenge to the parents, the psychiatrist, the psychologist, the educator, and the therapist. Our first concern is to try to form a relationship with him of trust and security, which he can accept as part of his environment. From his closed world he sends signals which we do not understand. Although he does not relate to people he often shows strange attachments to objects with which he identifies. Moreover he is not subnormal and may in fact possess concealed mental ability, or some special gift for mathematics, say, or music, or an incredible finger dexterity. Each autistic child is a unique individual. Our aim is to discover his musical personality and to build up with him a relationship through shared musical experiences, hoping that in the process he will develop a sense of purpose and achievement.

REACTIONS TO MUSIC

The way the autistic child relates to his environment is reflected in his reactions to music. Music or sound have the power to penetrate and may help to break down his defences, thus provoking communication. Music can create a non-verbal, non-threatening environment in which some kind of contact can be made, and in which the child can express himself. This contact can take many forms, sometimes very strange ones, for instance through the child's ritualistic approach to geometrical shapes which belong to a number of musical instruments such as the circular shape of a cymbal or a drum, the parallel lines formed by the row of strings on a violin or a cello, the rectangular pattern of a chime bar or a piano key, the layout of strings on an autoharp, the round hole of a pipe, the row of white and black keys on a keyboard. The autistic child often examines them with care, handles them, explores their tone, puts them on his lips, or even smears them with his saliva. Much of this is spontaneous. We have also to discover his awareness of certain musical elements and make use of it. I have worked with a child obsessed with unisons played on different instruments, another one who responded only to birds' songs, another one who could work only with two chime bars, neither more nor less.

All these and many others are part of the child's responses to a musical experience and are very revealing if he is left to do it in freedom. In offering him this experience we have to accept his bizarre behaviour and preferences which may be inexplicable. We have to observe his individual response to percussive, dissonant, or harmonious sounds. Therefore our musical approach to such a child has to be extremely flexible, within the framework of security, order, and predictability which he needs. If used with imagination, many of his rituals, symbols, and idiosyncrasies can become musically creative and be integrated in a musical experience. For instance, his obsession for wood can be gratified when he uses a wooden block and a mallet to produce rhythm. His interest in parallel lines can be used with an autoharp to produce perceptual contact, when he tries to pluck the strings. His sensitivity to musical resonance can be fed by the vibrations of a large cymbal or gong, with which he often identifies. Many autistic children relate to a particular instrument and its tone. But we have to take care that this identification is creative and not an opportunity for the child to isolate himself.

The following remarks from a child psychiatrist show a specialist's approach to the problem of music therapy:

With the autistic children it is necessary to use music in a strictly controlled situation because of their extreme sensitivity. Any direct attempt . . . meets with resistance, evasion and avoidance to the point that their fantasy life becomes essentially greater and they withdraw from reality more definitely. We therefore approach the problem as passively as possible by allowing the children to participate passively, actually listening and building their own fantasies, whatever they happen to be, in relation to the music. Gradually as reactions are observed it is possible to find the types of music to which the child seems to respond most satisfactorily and to build these into a semblance of organisation. At this point the child himself usually makes some effort at voluntary response. This may be a negative reaction in attempting to interfere with the organisation, or it may be positive, in which the child requests his own participation in the music session. In either case, by gradually getting his participation either negatively or positively, attempts are made to follow his emotional reactions as a means of self expression for the child. This takes considerable practice on the part of the music therapist and rather close relationship with the psychiatrist.[1]

LISTENING TO MUSIC

The autistic child is fascinated by any machine which makes noises, ticks, or revolves under his eyes. This affinity is well known, and can help us to give the child some musical experience through listening to a transistor or a cassette recorder held on his knees, and which he can see and, most important, touch.

[1] Eugene L. Aten, 'Psychiatric concepts in Music Therapy for Children'. *Music Therapy* (1953), pp. 85–87.

But nevertheless live music is best of all, unless the child refuses human contact. Here the musician has many opportunities to make experiments outside the conventional field, such as improvising.[2] The posture and the behaviour of an autistic child listening to music is often revealing. He may smile to himself, close his eyes, withdraw in himself, giggle or laugh. He may be stimulated by a strong rhythm or a sharp dissonance, or move and rock to a monotonous beat. These children who are upset by any change around them or frightened by the unexpected, are able to accept changes or the unexpected in music, and often seem actually to enjoy it. They react to many different kinds of music: classical forms such as minuets and bourrées, Spanish dances, pizzicato pieces, songs in foreign languages, lullabies, oriental music, and so on, provided that the music is within their span of attention. But we have also observed the strange affinity some of these children have for unorganized sounds, for instance long sounds played on open strings with the bow or long chordal lines as in choral or orchestral music. It is well known that autistic children can be reached by electronic or background film music. But not enough work has been done in this field to make any kind of generalization.

SELF-EXPRESSION

Most autistic children have little means of verbal expression, and suffer from lack or defects of speech. A number of them, however, can sing, hum to themselves, and remember songs. Those deprived of speech are able to utter sounds articulate enough to become rhythmical and expressive. Even with scanty vocal or instrumental means the autistic child can find some way to express his feeling or mood in music, be it violence, aggression, fear, disturbance, compulsion, resistance or chaos, and this can provide some emotional relief. Once the child has begun to let out his feelings we should help him to order the process, making him aware of the elements of sound he is using—intensity, pitch, duration, speed, tone colour, and

[2] Paul Nordoff and Clive Robbins, *Therapy in Music for Handicapped Children*, Gollancz, 1971.

so on. This is best done without words, with the musician playing a part related to the child's improvisation and helping him to find support in a harmony or a rhythm he can perceive. The child usually finds his own technique, and the more he remembers of the techniques, the better he is learning to express himself. The autistic child has little sense of achievement or motivation towards success. Even when he succeeds he seems to be indifferent to praise or to mastery, unless it is to please an adult. But even when his musical development is limited, its effect may reach very deep. Nevertheless I have dealt with a few children who possess an unexpected creative musical gift. They are able to improvise striking rhythms or beautiful harmonies on their various instruments. But their creations seem to be a self-contained form of self-expression, not to be shared with anyone.

LEARNING PROBLEMS

In music, as in other fields, we have to deal with the autistic child's learning problems and his abnormal use of cognitive or perceptual processes. We can also observe his adamant resistance to change, and the stereotyped automatic, rigid way he absorbs and accepts knowledge, which seems to be necessary to his sense of security. But in music we can to a certain extent avoid these obstacles by using an infinite variety of approaches to the learning situation: the same tune can be sung, or played on different instruments at different speed and intensity; a sequence of four notes can be reversed; the order of the series of chime bars is movable; the same rhythmic pattern can be clapped, beaten on a drum, plucked on a string; we can work sitting at a table or on the floor. The child is brought to accept a changing situation or techniques, within a secure environment. This difficult work cannot succeed until a stable, satisfactory relationship has been formed with the child. It may take a long time. When the child is not hospitalized, music sometimes can help to foster communication between the mother and the child within a non-threatening situation, and this can be beneficial to them both, especially when the mother is longing for some kind of contact at a higher level than the daily routine. We must be careful, however, to warn her not to expect a musical miracle.

GROUP WORK

Group work is a very difficult undertaking with truly autistic children since each of them lives in his own world. Some of them can achieve a good relationship with an adult, but rarely with another child. The music group may succeed when each of the children has become familiar with some common musical experience he can share with others. A common musical denominator has to be found. Singing is one of them, but only to a certain extent, since an autistic child can seldom sing well enough to join in with others. Movement to music is usually a satisfactory means, when each child can respond to the same rhythmical pattern, which he has absorbed; it must not be a monotonous beat which weakens awareness. The rhythmic pattern 'crotchet, crotchet, minim' seems to be the most effective one, as it can be verbalized rhythmically to accompany the corresponding action: hold my hand; lift your knees; stamp your feet, and so on, all phrases of one-syllable words. The music to accompany this collective activity is best improvised at the piano. It should be stimulating, played at a suitable tempo and mood. It should also contain moments of rest, immobility, and silence which the group has to control. The child engaged in a common activity is more likely to accept control and contact with others at a time when he feels free and happy.

The various techniques described in these chapters show that the music teacher or the therapist has to follow the immutable rule: namely that education or contact should be started at the child's own level, however low, and that we have to meet the child where he actually is. We may be able to make the autistic child respond to sound first and later to exteriorize his feelings, an experience which provokes his awareness of himself and the environment. In establishing contact we may give him a sense of security and satisfaction. We are trying to break through to an unfortunate child who is not yet part of our world, in the hope that, one day, he will belong.

9

THE CEREBRAL PALSIED CHILD

CEREBRAL palsy is in essence a disability of movement which affects many areas and impedes the physical, mental, and emotional development of the child at different degrees of severity. Nearly all cerebral palsied children suffer from some kind of speech or hearing defects; their limbs may be rigid, paralysed, or jerky; their spatial sense is defective and they often lack awareness of some part of their body. Many of them need the assistance of other people for the satisfaction of elementary needs such as toilet, dressing, feeding, or transport. As they feel insecure in a world fraught with dangers and difficulties they often lose the urge towards independence and adventure which is vital to a child's development, or they try to assert themselves in undesirable ways.

Many of them who suffer from lack of emotional and physical control give way to fits of anger or tantrums. Moreover, most of them are mentally retarded, and this adds to the many problems of their education and training.

SUITABLE TYPES OF MUSIC

A music programme for the cerebral palsied child should include the varied musical activities suitable to the child's physical, mental, and emotional state and rest on the conception that music is movement in space and time. Music can give the child the emotion of movement, because it moves in time and in space. Ascending and descending notes, as well as succession of sounds at different speeds and rhythms, can give a sensitive child the feeling of complete movement, up and down, slow or fast. In some cases music can even act as a substitute for movement, as in the instance of a cerebral palsied adolescent who was deprived of marching with others, but who was nevertheless able to play in the band and beat out the rhythm on his drum for those who could walk. This was a substitute which he was emotionally mature enough to accept and even to enjoy.[1] I have noticed that music expressing movement can deeply reach a child who is chair-bound or lying on his back, not only from his immediate response but from a transfer of this emotion into another means of expression. When cripple children make pictures inspired by a musical performance, they often express in the picture the emotion of movement which music has provoked in them, and this process seems to give them deep emotional satisfaction.

Cerebral palsied children react to many different kinds of music in a specific way. The general belief is that the cerebral palsied child needs soothing music to listen to, but at the same time when he makes music he is often given percussive rhythmical instruments on which he is allowed to play loudly, and this is a contradictory approach. In fact, musical activities and the kind of music used with cerebral palsied children should be related in principle to their medical diagnosis. Spastics and athetoids which are the two main groups of cerebral palsied children may respond in opposite ways to exciting or to soothing music. It may be a mistake to mix them in a listening or music-making group. Unfortunately the children are usually mixed during a music session, and unless one can find a common denominator music may not give all the good results one should hope for.

The two main types of music which produce spontaneous responses have been broadly classified by Dr. Thayer Gaston as physically stimulative and physically sedative:[2]

Stimulative music is the type that enhances physical energy, induces bodily activity, stimulates the striped muscles, the emotions and the subcortical reaction in man. It is based on such elements as strong rhythms, volume, cacophony and detached notes.

Sedative music is usually of a sustained, melodic nature in which strong rhythmic and percussive elements are lacking. This results in sedation, and responses of an intellectual and contemplative nature rather than physical.

These two types of music produce a psychosomatic effect of tension or relaxation which seems to affect differently the

[1] John D. McKee, *Two Legs to Stand On* (1955), p. 80.
[2] 'Dynamic Music Factors in Mood Change', *Music Educators Journal* (Spring 1951), p. 42.

spastic and the athetoid child. It has been observed during experiments made by Dr .E. Schneider[3] that the performance of a spastic child can become more controlled under the influence of stimulative music. The athetoid on the contrary can be greatly upset by the same music which provokes in him unwanted jerky movements. On the other hand, sedative music can help the performance of the athetoid and spoil that of the spastic.

During the experiment the children were asked to perform some tasks such as colouring geometrical patterns or putting pegs in a peg board. The music was played in the background, but some of the children selected for the test were quite conscious of the effect it had made on them.

As conscious listeners cerebral palsied children may respond primarily to rhythm. This can provoke a physical reaction which they may find difficult to control. Some cerebral palsied children react badly to stimulative music because it increases the feeling of tension and upsets them. For them the most suitable type of music is melodic, based on a regular and even pulse, played at a perceptible speed and nevertheless gay and lively. They are also sensitive to, and like, a musical tone lacking in intensity, as produced for instance on a recorder or on a muted string. Music containing sudden changes of speed, intensity, or rhythm is inadvisable with untrained cerebral palsied children. They are not able to adapt quickly and to control themselves, and may get frightened under too much stimulation. But if a cerebral palsied child is trained musically and becomes gradually accustomed to follow and to understand different moods in music even at an elementary level, he will enjoy a musical experience which has become familiar and lost its frightening aspect.

Playing an instrument or moving to music can assist the development of spatial judgement and motor control. The cerebral palsied child may be trained to become aware of a movement which should never be or become automatic. He should also be helped to form a mental picture of the movement producing the sounds associated with an emotion.

[3] 'Relationship between musical experiences and certain aspects of cerebral palsied children's performance', *Music Therapy* (1956), p. 250.

We should never forget that the essential value of music with a handicapped child consists in adding to his activities an indispensable element of emotion and enjoyment—an element which can transform or minimize the obstacles facing the child, whatever their nature or their degree. Nevertheless his emotional satisfaction when he tries to perform depends to a great extent on his ability to achieve certain movements, whether he plays or sings. Therefore the problem facing him is linked with his therapeutic treatment.

THERAPY

Music is sometimes used in physio- or speech-therapy, either for relaxation or stimulation, but the physical spontaneous response to music is too varied and too complex for the therapists to make full use of the dynamics of music, unless they possess specific musical knowledge. Nevertheless many of them use it with success at the obvious and superficial level. Music used in connexion with the treatment is usually recorded music, but music improvised at the time would bring much better results since it would follow the mood and the rhythm of the treatment at the right speed. The musician improvising at the piano may induce in the child a gradual transformation from a relaxed to an active mood when it is appropriate.

Certain enjoyable activities can be greatly helped by music because the music moving in time and space helps the child to regulate and to co-ordinate his movements. Weigl has observed that 'some cerebral palsied children achieve better results by rhythmical music and action songs. Movements such as stretching and bending, lowering the arms to the tempo and dynamics of an ascending and descending scale, personifying windmills, bicycle riders, or airplanes, can also be inserted in the music session.'[4]

INSTRUMENTS FOR THE CHILD TO PLAY

An American occupational therapist[5] has published a complete list of musical activities related to the treatment of the

[4] V. Weigl, 'Functional Music with Cerebral Palsied Children', *Music Therapy* (1954), p. 135.
[5] Barbara Denenholz, *Music Therapy* (1958), pp. 67–84.

cerebral palsied child. She describes the instrumental or vocal techniques that could help the child to increase his mobility, his range of motions, his endurance and power of co-ordination. She considers all parts of the body, and the co-ordination processes include eye-hand, eye-foot, hand-arm, and so on.

For instance, she has observed that to play at the extreme ends of keyboard instruments can help the movement of the shoulder-blades towards each other and activate the abductors and the elevators; and that the use of vertical chimes is beneficial when the child plays notes long enough for his arms to drop to the side of his body between strokes. This repeated movement helps to develop hand co-ordination and includes the process of grasping, reaching, and releasing. A method based on specially designed chimes has been tested and used successfully in special schools for cerebral palsied children in the State of California.[6] Miss Denenholz also points out that the muscles of the fingers which move the joints nearest to the wrist or second or third from the wrist can be exercised on some instruments such as the auto-harp, the guitar, or a woodwind instrument; similarly that singing soothing music can help to relax facial, palatal, and laryngeal muscles. She advocates the use of wind instruments to exercise the respiratory muscles and to improve breathing, and also in cases of defective mouth or dental formation.

Many objects have to be specially made or adapted for the use of the cerebral palsied child in view of his deficient grasp or lack of motor control, or his inability to sit or to stand erect. A musical instrument too may need to be adapted in order to provoke the right kind of physical movement and to improve motor control. In this case medical advice should be sought.

If the child has one good hand it should always be the activating one, and the weak one may be brought in quite unobtrusively. For instance, with cymbals or tambourines the weak hand becomes the 'helping hand'[7]—the helping hand may also be that of another child similarly affected, which helps social awareness and co-operation.

[6] Mynatt Breidentahl, *Music Therapy* (1958), pp. 87–93.
[7] Agatha H. Bowley, *The Young Handicapped Child* (1957), p. 70.

In his autobiography John D. McKee, born with spastic limbs, describes this process and its results. He was then a schoolboy:[8]

My drumming resulted from not being able to play the clarinet. . . . For a long time my left hand did all the work . . . with practice, however, my right hand become more useful and drumming gave that spastic hand more strength and direction than it had ever before . . . my right hand became responsive enough so that I could get a satisfactory roll out of a drum.

A number of drums or other instruments can be played sideways or downwards or even with the feet, thus providing a varied range of techniques, and giving the cerebral palsied child more opportunities to make music. The larger the instrument the easier it is to hit. Sticks used for hitting or beating are usually too thin for spastics, but they can easily be thickened to ensure the proper grasp from the thumb and fingers. Account should be taken of the general posture, including the position of the head and feet, as well as the use of the limbs. It is advisable to support the arms of the athetoid child in order to avoid as much as possible unwanted and jerky movements. Some instruments such as the dulcimer, the autoharp, or the chime bars can be placed on the tables specially made for the cerebral palsied child to learn to stand or to sit erect. One can also add visual aids to the instrument to help the child's spatial sense; for example, by placing a red dot on the target to be hit.

Instruments on which the strings can be strummed are particularly attractive to the cerebral palsied child; on some the strings can be plucked by all the fingers together, without moving individual fingers. The feel, sight, and sound of the vibrating string is extremely pleasant to the child because it results from a movement he has provoked. The use of strings of different colours may help him to direct his movements towards the right one. A one-string double bass may enable a cerebral palsied adolescent to join in the band, if he is able to pluck one note. Chime bars are useful in many ways, making single sounds or sequences of notes. They produce a deep effect on the child because of their lovely vibrating tone

[8] *Two Legs to Stand On*, pp. 75–76.

and also because of their pure intonation which plays an essential part in the emotional impact of any sound. They are melodic and percussive at the same time and can be used extensively in group or individual work.

Some instruments can be played in a lying down position, especially simple wind instruments such as bamboo pipes. Blowing and producing a sound with one's mouth is the next thing to the voice, and may deeply satisfy a child who is frustrated by a speech defect. Moreover, the use of a wind instrument develops awareness of lips and tongue movements. The use of a simple wind instrument may produce the same physical results as the blowing exercises used in speech therapy when the child blows through a small tube to move a feather lying on a flat surface, and the process may be emotionally more satisfying. Music can be used in speech therapy as a means of relaxation of tension. 'Music', says Charles P. Pedry,[9] 'may be used to advantage in helping the cerebral palsied child to relax. This relaxation in turn makes it easier for the child to better produce the sounds which the speech therapist is trying to teach him.'

Teachers, doctors, and psychologists are usually much impressed by the level of physical performance of cerebral palsied children when they try to make music, not only by the unexpected standard of their motor control but also by their unusual span of attention. Normally the cerebral palsied child is afraid of movement which represents to him a source of failure and threatening experiences. This fear increases his tension and his motor disability. Moreover, much of his distractibility may be due to nervous instability which prevents him from concentrating and settling on one object. But music-making can fix the interest of the child and divert his attention from his disability and fear of movement by focusing it on the enjoyment of singing or playing an instrument. In this way we can help the child to by-pass or override his emotional fear. Music-making should make him less aware of his handicap and with a feeling of success he may gradually become conscious of the movement required to sing or to play and even

[9] *Music Therapy* (1959), p. 81.

try to improve it. During this slow process he may even gain a mental image of the movement focused on the musical instrument and forget his disability. Joan Saunders and Marjorie Napier refer to Professor Plum's emphasis on 'the importance in all exercise of making the child *think* about every movement. If a movement should become automatic the doing of it cannot make new pathways in the damaged brain, therefore all movements should be varied in speed, strength of resistance and so on.'[10]

These remarks are concerned with more than physical exercises, but they apply equally well to musical activities. The child who makes music has to prepare and to 'think' his movement in order to strike or to blow at the right moment. In this way music can help him to regulate his movement according to musical time and to form in his mind an image of the movement he is about to make. The cerebral palsied child cannot improve his playing unless he is mentally aware of his movement. Moreover, automatic movement cannot create emotion and indeed is likely to kill the benefit that the child could gain from expressing himself in music.

SINGING

I have described at some length the use of musical instruments for the cerebral palsied child because it is directly related to his specific disability of movement.[11] But the cerebral palsied child is not always physically able to handle an instrument, and even if he could do so there are a few cases where such activity is undesirable as it may increase nervous tension or hyperactivity. But music can offer the cerebral palsied child a more spontaneous and natural way to express himself, namely singing. Singing should be in the forefront of the musical activities of the cerebral palsied child, whether he can handle a musical instrument or not. When the child sings, he expresses himself and at the same time can keep his limbs completely passive, the arms relaxed, and falling on the side

[10] *Spastics in Cheyne Walk* (1957), p. 90.
[11] J. Alvin, 'Music and the Handicapped Child', *Spastics' Quarterly* (December 1963), pp. 36–47.

of his body. This feeling of relaxation at the time he is expressing himself is a rare one for him. Much patience and skill are required to teach singing to cerebral palsied children, many of whom growl or have little control of their voice.

A number of cerebral palsied children attempt to sing words they cannot speak, and sometimes succeed. This should give them some confidence in their verbal ability, help them to remember words and possibly help to decrease the emotional tension they experience when they try to verbalize and are frustrated.

The benefit the cerebral palsied child derives from singing is quite irrespective of his standard of performance, and he should be encouraged to try and persevere so long as he does not unduly disturb the group. The teacher should avoid any social problem within the group since singing together should be a happy and creative occupation (see p. 59).

We may conclude by saying that the various forms of tension produced by cerebral palsy affect the whole individual in his mind, body, and emotions, and may prevent the child from realizing himself, even if he possesses a good intelligence. Through music he can express himself, gain some awareness of movement, and at the same time experience physical and emotional release. This is the specific contribution that music can make, and a valuable one.

10

THE DELICATE CHILD—
THE PHYSICALLY HANDICAPPED
CHILD

THERE are two main groups of children suffering from physical handicaps and whose educational potentials are normal or near normal: the delicate children and the physically handicapped children, for whom special education is provided.

Delicate children suffer from various, sometimes incurable, physical disorders such as a weak heart, asthma, diabetes, or others which impair their general development. Many of them are under some medical treatment which disrupts their schooling as much as the disorder itself. They are difficult to bring up and to educate. Their continual concern for their health may become obsessive or morbid, and their symptoms are distressing to themselves and to others. Although the teacher should be sympathetic and understanding he should not protect them too much or make too much allowance for their disability.

VARIOUS PROBLEMS

Although he suffers from low stamina the delicate child may possess intelligence and imagination. Music is an admirable means to activate him without undue exertion. He should be offered concrete musical experiences, since he often tries to escape from a world too strong and too demanding for him. He may as a performer or a listener enjoy music and discover in it a source of dynamism and strength, either in the experience itself or because it adds life and interest to other subjects. Since he gets easily tired, and cannot keep attentive for long, some of the techniques described in other chapters apply to him as well (see pp. 45, 75, 85).

The physically handicapped child is a cripple who has lost the use of some part of his body. Either he has been born a cripple—like the unfortunate thalidomide babies—or he has met with an accident or an illness which has left him maimed for life. In the latter case he may remember the traumatic experience and finds it very difficult to adapt to his new condition. This child is in need of rehabilitation in the full sense of the word. With the other child born already affected we meet a different problem of acceptance similar to that of the cerebral palsied child.

Children suffering from severe physical disability require special care, apparatuses, and treatment, and are often cared for in residential schools. There music can function at its best, since it is possible to integrate it with the whole life of the child. In such a school the music teacher can fully answer the challenge and plan musical activities suitable to each of the children in his care.

SELF-EXPRESSION

A number of physically handicapped children possess a normal intelligence and a certain physical dynamism which should find as many outlets as possible. When the cripple is mentally active and emotionally stable it is imperative that he should be asked to produce satisfactory musical results at a reasonable musical standard set up by the teacher. He must feel that his handicap does not prevent him from being as good as a normal child in music, and he should be given the suitable means to achieve it. Cripples owe much of their achievement to their admirable courage and perseverance. The musical field is of particular value to them because it brings as well an emotional reward.

The most striking case I have seen among many others was a boy of twelve born without legs. He had two normal arms, but the right hand was missing and replaced by an orthopaedic hook; his only hand was a shapeless stump with two fingers. In spite of this appalling handicap he was of average intelligence, very sociable, and had a lovely sensitive face. Music had become the centre of his life. He had learned the trumpet, the only instrument he could manage, holding it with the hook and pressing on the keys with his fingers. He had been well taught and was a much appreciated member of the senior orchestra. His love of music was obvious from the expression on his face when he was playing or listening to music.

One of the striking features of an orchestra of physically handicapped children, irrespective of their standard of performance, is the way they manage to express movement in music. Music-making seems to answer a deep need which must express itself in spite of their infirmity.

Special orthopaedic devices or attachments can enable a crippled child to play an instrument, such as the fitting of a bow to an artificial arm, or a simple lever which enables him to use the piano pedal through a movement of the waist. Many of the techniques are similar to those described in the chapter on the cerebral palsied, who is also a crippled child.

11

THE CHILD WITH A SENSORY HANDICAP

THE BLIND CHILD

MUSIC with the blind child seems so obvious that the following pages may be thought unnecessary. Nevertheless, there is much to be said on the subject.

The blind child, like the deaf, is a deprived and frustrated being who lacks one of the essential sensory means of development and communication. The blind are often supposed to possess an exceptional auditory faculty, but this is only partly true. Nature does not endow the blind child with a better hearing apparatus, but his handicap does force him to develop, sometimes to an uncanny extent, an exceptional ability to listen. All means that can contribute towards the development of this ability are valuable, since most of his contacts with the world depend on his perception and interpretation of sound.

COMMUNICATION

These contacts also depend on his sense of touch. The tactile sensibility developed as a result can be valuable when it comes to playing a musical instrument. In fact, the blind child is often better equipped in this respect than a normal child. Moreover, blindness does not impair the movements required to play a musical instrument, since they do not exceed the length of the arms. Therefore the blind child can use space freely, without being afraid of meeting an obstacle as he does when he moves about. The process helps him to form a mental concept of his body in relation to his instrument, and this is a further step towards his physical integration with his surroundings. He also benefits greatly from music and movement (see pp. 145–6).

Except for the fact that lack of vision is a material impediment, there is no reason why a blind child should not do in music as well, if not better than a normal child. His awareness and memory of sound, his attention when he listens, make him respond readily to music. A blind child may not be by nature more sensitive to music, but he soon becomes so because music can fulfil many of his emotional, intellectual, and social needs. He is ready to enjoy musical experiences as a listener and as a performer.

The blind child, being unable to see, has little sense of security. He may react badly, with fear or withdrawal, to strange places or a change of routine. To counter this he should be presented with situations in which he can feel secure in spite of his disability. He should also be encouraged to develop self-confidence through some kind of achievement which can give him faith in himself and a feeling of stability. He should also, whenever and as early as possible, acquire skills and interests which he could still pursue in adult life. For all these needs music can provide an answer.

The child's fundamental need is for communication which gives security and has meaning. From the day the blind infant becomes aware of sound, music should play a part in his development. Already at the pre-verbal level, music can give the child a feeling for organized and rhythmical sounds that have continuity. A blind child, more than any other, can benefit from learning songs at an early age because this trains his own voice to be meaningful, harmonious, and expressive. Much normal human communication depends not only on words, but on tone of voice and facial expression, mostly from the eyes. Blind eyes are not expressive and cannot convey feelings. Moreover, many of our facial expressions are acquired through imitation, and the blind child cannot imitate what he has not seen. But a voice can carry as much meaning as the face or the eyes do. The blind child should be trained to use his vocal apparatus as an expressive instrument to compensate for this deficiency.

PERFORMING AND READING

The blind child can express himself fully through music, as any other child does, but techniques have to be adapted to his handicap. If such a child is particularly gifted he may even become a professional musician. There are many fine examples of remarkable performers or composers who have conquered their blindness and led a truly creative life. But even without aiming at such high achievements music can become the life pursuit of the blind if he has received the full training necessary for success. There are a number of blind piano tuners and even music teachers, mostly in schools for the blind, who are valuable members of the community.

Music is also, at any age, a group activity in which the blind can take part if he is able either to memorize his part or to read it in Braille music notation. He should learn to read music like any other child. He should be able to sing and read his part at the same time, provided that the sheet is securely placed under his hand for him to follow his part easily. The process is more difficult when he plays an instrument since one hand has to be used for reading. Certain instruments can be adapted to a one-hand technique or supplemented with a foot pedal replacing one hand, especially percussion instruments such as drums, tambourines, cymbals, castanets, triangles, or others. This enables the blind child to take part in an instrumental music group without having to play by rote.

I have already mentioned that a child who cannot read music makes only limited progress. This applies to the blind child as well. He should learn to read and write Braille music notation in order not to depend entirely on his musical memory and on the help of others. The individual teaching of parts by rote is not always practical and often very tedious. Moreover, the ability to read a text contributes to the whole intellectual development of the child, whether the text is words or music. The mental interpretation of sounds through a combination of written symbols follows the same process in the Braille system as in the normal visual method. The blind child who can master Braille music notation is able to read the part allotted to him, or to take down any tune he hears, just as well as a seeing child; or even to compose. At a higher level it can also help him to become familiar with music written in Braille. Whatever level he attains, this achievement is beneficial to the blind child in many ways. It enables him to be self-reliant, since he can study on his own, and this answers his deep need for independence which should be fulfilled whenever possible.

Moreover, the blind child often enjoys the intellectual side of music which includes ear training, music appreciation, history of music, or any subject allied to music. Music then may become a deep and rich experience related to a wide field of culture.

The education of any handicapped child should open to him a life as broad as possible, and prevent him from turning inwards or sinking into himself. A sensory handicap such as blindness or deafness can easily make the child become ego-centric since he is so very dependent in a world of people who can see or hear and he may tend to live in himself. Very often a blind child develops tics and mannerisms of which he is not aware, such as rocking or making grimaces to himself. Musical activities can make him communicate with a world in which he is fully involved. Music can thus help him to become part of the environment he cannot see and divert his attention from himself. At the same time he can identify with the music and project his personality through an enjoyable means of expression at his level (see p. 32).

The blind child may become a good performer as well as a good listener. There exist a number of good choirs of blind children or adults who perform in public with a conductor who is not there to be seen, but to be felt by the singers as the focal-point towards which they project their voice. Most schools for the blind do excellent choral work and possess a large repertoire because of the special auditory memory that the blind child possesses. The value of group activity is at least as great with the blind as with any other child, and their achievements in choral work should be more fully recognized.

There is no reason why a blind child could not learn to play a musical instrument, provided that he possesses enough general ability and musical aptitude. He can learn the recorder, the piano, or any other instrument if he is able to train his musical memory. He cannot always play an instrument and read Braille notation at the same time.

The teacher has to adapt his methods and teach the child how to integrate and memorize auditory, tactile, and kinesthetic experiences without any visual help. The child who can see is shown how to use his hands and imitates what he sees. The blind child can imitate only what he hears. A second piano in the room is very useful on which the teacher plays what the child should do once he knows how to place his fingers on the keys, and the same method applies to the teaching to the blind of any instrument.

The blind child needs much concentration to learn the technique, and his efforts should be carefully graded in order to avoid frustration, and to give him satisfaction without strain. But the spontaneous pity aroused by blindness should not prevent the teacher from making on the child the normal demands that bring progress. Only then can the child gain a sense of achievement, and learn enough to express himself in music and integrate with his instrument.

SENSITIVENESS TO SOUND

Although it is better to treat the blind child as a normal one, the teacher should be much aware of the great sensitiveness of a child who is specially vulnerable and dependent. The teacher should offer him only experiences in which he can feel secure, understood, and trusted to do well. We musicians should also remember that the child who lives in a world of sound is bound to be acutely affected by it—and that sound may even be to him a source of strain or nervous fatigue. Music should provide him with a means of relaxation in which sounds become familiar, not threatening, and shaped in a harmonious and predictable form. This alone is bound to bring him much emotional release.

The blind child can experience through listening to music all the joys of a normal child; they may even be of a more musical kind. The young blind child does not live in the animistic world where inanimate things live and move—he has no visual imagination and music cannot evoke pictures in his mind. Music to him is an emotional experience not related to vision. For that reason, music may be more effective and reach him more deeply because it does not stop at the level of visual association.

Music can express to the blind, as to any other child, only experiences with which he is familiar, and none of them is of a visual kind. Nevertheless he can respond in his own way to the basic elements of music, for example to rhythm and speed that express familiar movements; tone colour that gives the sensation of texture and of tactile perceptions such as softness, hardness, resilience, or angularity; contrasts in pitch or rhythm that convey an auditive effect of surprise or excitement; intensity or volume which give an impression of plenitude or distance; and so on. The blind child may also find in music feelings, emotions, and moods to which he can relate and respond with his whole being, as well, and perhaps better than a normal child. He may be reached more deeply by the spiritual element in music because he relates it to fewer concrete experiences.

Music can make a unique contribution to the life of the child deprived of vision, without any of the reservations attached to other handicaps. Music may be to the blind child a complete means of self-expression through which he can communicate and integrate socially. Moreover, because of his sensitive response to sound, he can find in music a source of spiritual and cultural values which may greatly contribute to his happiness and welfare.

THE DEAF CHILD

Music in the education of the deaf child seems to be a paradoxical proposition—but it is in fact accepted by specialists and psychologists at a scientific and experimental level. Many schools for the deaf use music with good results.

Deafness may consist in a total loss of hearing either congenital from birth or through illness or accident later in life. The attitude towards sound of the child who has experienced hearing and of the child who is only partially deaf is very different from that of the child totally deaf from birth, and this should be taken into account by the music teacher. In any case deafness creates a more or less severe loss of relationship with the environment which impairs the learning process and can alter in a drastic way the personality of the child. It is difficult to imagine the wall of silence that surrounds the growing deaf child and the continuous feeling of isolation he must suffer from. Sound accompanies all living development and is so much integrated in our environment that very often we do not perceive it consciously. What we call silence is only relative, and we speak of a 'dead silence' to express a complete absence of life.

Consciously or unconsciously from our birth we learn through the sounds that surround us. Our normal means of communication is through the verbal sounds that we first perceive and then imitate. Reading and writing that follow are only spatial symbols of sound.

Deafness is a grave handicap to the learning process, since it impairs or prevents the acquisition of language and the development of concepts. It is also a barrier to social contacts and group activities which more or less depend on verbal communication. A deaf child often looks stupid or retarded although he is not, but he is unable to respond to the stimulus of sound. In his soundless world the deaf child can easily become withdrawn, depressed, or neurotic unless means can be found to bring him out of his isolation.

SOUND VIBRATIONS

Sound to normal people is an auditory perception, but the waves produced by a vibrating body and transmitted to us through air can reach us by other means. They can be felt through the skin and bones which are not part of the auditory apparatus. This perception cannot be compared with what we hear, but it enables the deaf child to be in contact with the surrounding world of sound that moves through time. He can even apprehend some of its elements such as rhythm, accentuation, pitch, loudness, and duration. This is limited, but positive, and one can build on this perception quite a programme of development.

The normal child develops a sense of body rhythm mostly

through his sense of hearing. He learns to move according to a pattern of rhythmical sounds regulated by an experience denied to the deaf child.

There has been some interesting controversy about the conditioning of body rhythm through the continuous and unconscious absorption of sound patterns. The question arose whether a child totally deaf from birth could respond spontaneously to rhythmical sounds if he was made suddenly to perceive them. Although some training is necessary for him to respond, it seems in fact that the deaf child who has not yet been exposed to music *is* sensitive to the physical stimulus of rhythm once he can apprehend it

The lack of response to rhythmical stimulus is often observed in the aphasic child who is not deaf, although he often seems to be. The absence of response to a stimulus does not mean necessarily that there has been no experience: it may be that the mechanism through which the response should be made is defective. But the deaf child is not aphasic, and we should try to stimulate and to cultivate by all means his responses to music, however weak. Most of his responses are through movement which is his natural form of expression.

Hearing aids are a new and wonderful device that often transform the life of a deaf child and are a valuable help towards his development. These apparatuses which increase the deaf child's perception of sound have given a special place to music in the education of the deaf child. There are today very few children who are 100 per cent deaf, thanks to the work of scientists such as I. R. and A. W. G. Ewing[1] and others. The apparatuses carry or amplify the sounds to the deaf child. Some are worn individually by the children who learn to control them, others are placed in the room for group work. They help to increase or decrease the volume or intensity of the music to the suitable level—or they put the emphasis on certain parts or ranges which are perceptible to the child. The music teacher should be conversant with the use of these hearing aids.

It is often difficult for the deaf child, even wearing a hearing

[1] *New Opportunities for Deaf Children* (1958).

aid, to locate the direction of sound; this is why a live performance may sustain his attention better than a recorded one. Moreover, the music should be in the lower register and with a strong bass since the deaf child is likely to respond better to low frequency sounds. The low sounds of a strong rhythmical bass may give the deaf child his first impression of rhythm in time and an opportunity to translate it into movement (see p. 145).

Before the use of hearing aids severely deaf children trying to dance to music usually could only imitate the movements made by the teacher facing them, and the pianist had to follow. Today many of them can respond spontaneously to the rhythm of the sounds and move to it; a free kinesthetic experience which has a completely different significance, since it is creative and comes from the child himself.

I have several times mentioned the therapeutic principle that we should build on what already exists in the child and bring it out into consciousness. This principle can also be applied to the deaf child. He does not apprehend sound vibrations as we do, so, as well as exposing him to the stimulus of sound from outside, we should make him produce the sound himself. In this way he is involved enough to become conscious of the cause and effect. He may not listen as a normal child does, but when he acts on the vibrating body he himself creates a circle of stimuli and responses which helps his awareness and makes him more conscious of and more receptive to the vibrations he is provoking. For instance, clapping the rhythm, hitting a tambourine, shaking a bell, or blowing in an instrument can train the child to make a sound of which he becomes conscious in some way, and that others can hear.

AWARENESS OF SOUND

The awareness of the vibrations of sound gives much pleasure to the deaf child, especially if he has provoked it himself. The deaf infant should play with musical toys which may give him not only an opportunity to perceive certain sounds, but also a means of producing sounds he is able to apprehend. We have already discussed the infants' exploration of sound, but purely in terms of auditory perception. Here we try to provoke in the deaf child the awareness of a world in which the vibrations of sound can be apprehended and enjoyed through different means, even if they are not perceived in a normal way. Once the deaf child can feel sound vibrations and apprehend their rhythm, he has acquired a precious means of development.

USE OF CERTAIN INSTRUMENTS

With the deaf as with any other handicapped child we have first to assess at which level we can start and to find out the technique through which we can reach him and contribute to his growth. He can feel the vibrations of sound through his skin or his bones. He may be helped by some hearing aids fixed to his head and in contact with his skull. Other deaf children feel the vibrations through other parts of their body, for instance through their hands resting on the resounding body of a musical instrument such as the piano, or through their feet, if they move to music on a special floor which transmits the vibrations. Many deaf children love to play the auto-harp, not because of its tone, but because they hold it on their lap and can feel the vibrations through their whole body. Some teachers have obtained good results with the accordion. The tambourine, which expresses rhythm, can convey much to the deaf child, since he can place the instrument against any part of his body, head, cheek, throat, or hand, and feel it vibrate when he drums on it. He can also walk or dance with it as it is a portable instrument. High-pitched instruments are rarely suitable; most deaf children cannot perceive high sounds; but their whole body seems to be sensitive to low sounds which give them a feeling of volume or plenitude.

Some deaf children can apprehend large intervals between the notes although it is not possible for a normal person to imagine the kind of effect contrasts in pitch can make on them. Some specialists have even been able to make some deaf children appreciate differences in pitch as small as one tone, but this was after a long training.

The piano, which is a large sounding case, can be used to

give the deaf child his first experience in organized rhythm and in contrasts in pitch. The child, his eyes closed, leaning on or putting his hand on the piano, is able to get a message through another sense perception and to respond to it in a creative way.

The deaf child can be trained to perceive sound vibrations, to apprehend and to remember their logical organization through rhythm. Some teachers make the young child 'feel' the rhythmical vibrations of the piano and then let him interpret their mood in running, skipping, or marching. Later on the child can be asked to tap a rhythm he has perceived. When he has memorized it, he can leave the piano and move to that specific rhythm. He returns to the piano in order to refresh his memory or to get another rhythm. Little by little he can recognize, memorize, and name different simple rhythms such as a waltz or a march, which he is able to interpret through movement without having to return to the piano. Some establishments for the deaf have special rooms fitted with magnetic loops and a resilient wooden floor through which the children can perceive the vibrations in all parts of the room where they dance to the music. Their physical reactions are as fast as those induced by a purely auditory process, and an uninitiated spectator may not be aware that the dancers are deaf.

This creative activity is one of the most valuable and effective ways for the deaf child to enjoy social contacts and to share in a group activity in which he may express himself among people who can hear. This helps him to gain confidence in himself.

SPEECH

The deaf child learning to speak is greatly helped by developing a feeling for rhythm and rhythmical patterns. He can relate the accentuation of words to the accentuation in music and although he cannot sing he is able to connect a rhythmical pattern of a few chords with a word or a sentence accentuated in the same way (for instance: PO TA TO and

♩ ♩ ♩). This can help him to get a better concept of verbal

rhythm and may enable him to participate in choral activities once he has acquired a feeling for a sequence of differently accentuated sounds. His participation resembles the monotone part sung by the mentally retarded growler, but this is due to very different causes.

SELF-EXPRESSION

Music to the deaf child cannot be an aesthetic and emotional experience as such, because even at his best he is deprived of the perception of certain elements indispensable to the emotional impact of music, namely tone colour and harmony. Moreover, he cannot perceive the whole range of notes and appreciate the affective meaning of intervals. Nevertheless there is a strong emotional factor at work in music for the deaf child. It can create communication which is already an emotional experience to an isolated child—it can give him a sense of rhythm which enlarges his conception of the perceptual world—it can give him means to express himself joyfully through movement. When he moves to music with others who perhaps can hear, he can communicate through an experience shared in pleasure and happiness. If he can manage to make sounds on a musical instrument, he may even participate in a music-making group. Some deaf children can join in general activities of this type, among spastics, retarded, or even normal children.

Music used with patience and knowledge can help to break up the inhibitions and the feeling of inferiority from which so many deaf children suffer. If these depressing feelings are allowed to grow, the deaf child becoming an adult may not be able to face his handicap. Any means that enable the deaf child to express himself among others and to integrate in his community are of the greatest value to his mental health, to the development of his personality, and can transform his life as an adult. But if music is to be one of these means, the music teacher should possess the infinite patience that comes from love and understanding and also the knowledge needed for an exacting and rewarding task.

12

MUSIC AND MOVEMENT

MOVEMENT is so closely allied to music that both can be integrated in one experience. It is not easy to discern whether movement interprets music or vice versa, and I do not propose to examine the relative value to the handicapped child of the many schools concerned with music and movement. I shall discuss movement only as a response to a musical stimulus in relation to a handicap.

THE PHYSICALLY HANDICAPPED AND THE CEREBRAL PALSIED CHILD

These children suffer from obvious impediments, but with the help of music they can enjoy the physical ability they still possess and make the best use of it. They suffer from lack of body rhythm and poor co-ordination of movement. They may benefit more from having their instinctive responses to music directed at once towards conscious and meaningful movements. These children usually gain by moving as rhythmically as possible, and this should not prevent them from using their imagination and expressing themselves.

Music and movement does not consist only in moving the whole body. A physically handicapped child, unless he is totally deprived of movement can express something through any controllable motion. To the immobile child indeed, musical games and activities are precious and valuable. For instance, 'finger' games in which each finger becomes an individual and expresses something different; mime in which movements of the head and facial expression alone may follow and express a musical theme. These means and many others can give the cripple some kinesthetic sensation and help him to use the physical means he possesses, however restricted.

I have conducted or attended many sessions of movement to music with physically handicapped children, even with crippled children in wheel chairs. They turned round and round to a waltz, let off steam, and then relaxed happily. All the children wore on their face a look of excited satisfaction and gratification which sometimes amounted almost to ecstasy. In those and other cases, music and movement was used as an emotional safety valve of a completely non-intellectual nature. This kind of experience is not disorganized; it is not yet organized; it has not got out of control; it is not yet controlled. This does not mean that in time it cannot become controlled and orderly.

We can find much material suitable to the young physically handicapped child. With the adolescent, the work presents the same problems that have been discussed in other chapters, namely the discrepancy that exists between the child's emotional maturity and the limitations imposed by his mental or physical condition. A physical handicap, unless it is small, curtails the participation in physical activities outside the school where adaptation can be made. Handicapped adolescents still at school may try to dance to music within their group, and in their own way. The motivation is sometimes so strong that I have seen attempts at 'twist' from children wearing calipers. When these attempts are physically harmless they should be encouraged, if only to give the child the joy in movement that is so valuable for mental balance. But little by little, the physically maimed adolescent may realize that he cannot move to music and participate in a group of normal adults. There is no other solution except through a substitute. I have already quoted the case of the lame school-leaver who beat the drums when the other boys were marching. He learnt how to enjoy a substitute that made up for his inability and enabled him to be part of movement to music (see p. 113).

Physically handicapped children are seldom able to make harmonious movements, but they should try to move smoothly and to follow a continuous line. Percussive music is not always inducive of harmony of movement; it often upsets motor co-ordination because of its precision in time which is very demanding. In that case music with a strong melodic line may be more successful.

THE MENTALLY SUBNORMAL CHILD

Our approach to music and movement with the retarded child should be quite different. We have to take into consideration his mental age, his poverty of physical awareness, his inability to generalize and to concentrate, his apathy or hyperactivity. He is usually responsive to music in an unsophisticated, primitive way, but cannot be expected to coordinate music and movement before he has reached a mental age of at least three when he may become aware of the process. Any work with the retarded child has to be adapted to his power of learning and his span of attention. In music and movement we can use methods which work at a low intellectual level such as imitation, automatism, and repetition, provided that the child is motivated enough to imitate and to repeat.

The severely subnormal child can be helped to develop a spatial sense by making movements corresponding to a specific musical pattern repeated again and again; for instance, by drawing large circles on a blackboard when music making a circular effect is being played. This device has been used as a first step towards learning to write, and the child derives a pleasurable incentive from it.

All education of the mentally retarded child aims at developing his awareness and understanding of relationship. When he moves to music he becomes conscious of his body in relation to the music and his surroundings. Moreover, it may give him the physical balance which he lacks even when he is physically fit. Though his responses to music and movement may be of a primitive kind they can become meaningful in the process. Even at a low level moving to music requires a certain amount of mental work since there is a connexion between the music heard and the movement that responds. This movement can express a feeling or a mood, or picture a mental image, an improvisation by the child at the level of his own experiences. The teacher should help him to make use of many different movements corresponding to the music. First, movements using space, but without moving about, from the arms or legs, bending or stretching, in which the child's body is the central point from which movement radiates. Symmetrical movements are easier for him to perform than asymmetrical ones that require better motor control, therefore a duple rhythm is easier for him to follow than a triple one. Music should help to make more harmonious the movements which the child makes in daily life such as walking, bending, jumping, or running, kneeling or lying down. Holding a real or imaginary object— not necessarily a musical instrument—gives significance and reality to a movement.

Smaller movements can give the child some awareness of a specific part of his body and help him to build up gradually his 'body image'. For instance, hands can become expressive not only when the child claps the rhythm but when he opens or closes his fingers or uses his fist in response to the music. Specially devised exercises or games can give the child a feeling for his whole foot, or his toes or his heels, or his elbow, that can be put into action.

Music should be extremely simple but characteristic enough for the child to be struck by a dominant element that may provoke in him a specific movement and if possible at the right speed.

We have to find out what the child's spontaneous response to music is likely to be in order to work first on what is already in the child. As we have seen, his initial response may be to rhythm, to intensity or volume, to pitch or tone colour and so on. This response may be either his own or an imitation of what others are doing around him. This often happens in a group and may mislead the teacher on the child's ability to respond individually.

The child's spontaneous response may be musical enough to need no added stimulus. The child who is able to make his own pattern of movements needs only guidance towards an organization of these movements. Other children may want another stimulus, for instance they may only be able to imitate, and move with, the teacher; or they may need the help of a suggestion or a musical image, and be told that the music plays a windmill, a tree, a woodpecker, or a toy. At first the best image is one suggesting only one kind of rhythmical repetitive movement. As we have seen in other chapters, a repetitive movement loses its monotonous character when a musical element is added to it, that gives meaning and continuity: for instance, an increase or decrease in volume or in speed, or a harmonic sequence that brings the movement to a conclusion. The woodpecker's tapping may become louder and louder—the windmill may turn slower and slower or the doll may go to sleep.

All these means can be enlarged and follow the development of the child's awareness and physical control. We can then try to interpret feelings through movement, and make the child conscious of harmonious movements expressing the mood of the music. Gay and light-hearted music provokes light movements such as skipping or bouncing. A retarded child may not be able to reproduce strictly certain musical rhythms such as ♫ for skipping, but he may catch the character of the music and keep to the general beat.

The retarded child can grasp contrasts in pitch, high and low notes that provoke stretching up, bending, or kneeling down movements. These can be purposeful, expressive, and harmonious, such as reaching for the moon, or drinking from the brook—or in a different mood picking apples from the tree or gathering windfalls, movements that stop when the music comes to an end and the basket is full.

Movements to music can be devised for all stages of maturity, experience, and intelligence. The adolescent can be given adult themes to match the type of music that appeals to him. Again, we should be guided by the way he responds emotionally to music.

When the child has acquired a repertoire of movements and can respond spontaneously to some musical stimulus, well defined and characteristic, we can try to give him more complex tasks, to provoke more involved movements which require an increasing amount of motor control and memory. The music also should become more complex, provided that his auditory discrimination has improved. A backward child told me once that in 'The Swan' by Saint-Saëns she had heard the music make a picture at three different levels. The 'cello part described the swan moving on the pond, the ripples on the water were heard in the piano part, and underneath, deep down in the bass, she could detect the low propelling movements of the bird's feet. That child felt music as movement and her description, although clumsy, made a complete picture of a harmonious and rhythmical swimming process.

When the mentally handicapped child is able to memorize simple steps of a repetitive kind he finds a whole field of traditional dances open to him. Retarded boys and girls can partake in an activity which may also be shared with normal children. This dancing can become quite an occasion, when the children wear traditional and national costumes to fit the part. They can contribute to school shows and integrate socially at quite an adult level. Such opportunities whenever possible should not be lost in E.S.N. schools or even in training centres. The experience may help the retarded child who is not able to handle musical instruments with the necessary skill. But he may find in his own body moving to music an instrument of self-expression and a creative activity that is emotionally and socially satisfying.

THE MALADJUSTED CHILD

The retarded child lacks rhythm through mental deficiency and bad muscular co-ordination. The emotionally disturbed child lacks inner rhythm because of his unstable, chaotic condition. The retarded child is ready to accept rhythm from outside, the disturbed child may refuse its message of order and harmony because he is a rebel. But music and movement offer him such an attractive emotional outlet that, left to himself, he may not resist it. This opportunity to move to music should be given to him unobtrusively and even silently. The music to which he moves at last follows certain rules, which are bound in the end to affect him.

The technique should aim at creating in the disturbed child a feeling of release through a kinesthetic activity which has form and order. The experience should be presented to him in a way he is likely to accept, at his level of intelligence and maturity. The imagination of the disturbed child is often vivid but volatile; any suggestion made by the music should be followed up immediately and put into action. The musical theme should be characteristic and persuasive enough to sustain the child's attention. With the volatile child each part of the music session should be as short as possible and end before the child loses interest. The child would gain more from the musical experience if he could be induced first to listen to a short musical item before moving to it instead of plunging at once into a world of fantasy. He may also prefer to follow his inspiration instead of being prompted by the teacher or the title of the musical piece. Nevertheless the teacher should try to make him regulate his movements in order to fit in as well as possible with the melody or the pulse of the music, or to personify better the character he is supposed to be. In any case some control should develop directed towards a better integration with the music.

This kind of approach may succeed with an extroverted, imaginative child. But the withdrawn, inhibited, and suspicious child may resist responding to music and refuse to move. He may also be frightened and it may take him a long time before he shows any physical reaction to music. But we can work patiently on its primitive appeal, on the child's curiosity, on his desire to imitate or on any other means which may provoke a reaction. He may still be too shy, too much afraid of being watched, to move with other children. But music itself may give him the sense of security and support he needs to lose his inhibition and join the group. Social integration through music and movement follows the same process as through making music, which we have already discussed.

The disturbed, withdrawn child gains from music and movement even more than the extrovert type who always finds acceptable or even unacceptable ways of self-expression. The introvert and secretive child lives in his own world; what he feels, what he thinks, should be brought out through means appealing to him and which he will not resist. He may discover in music and movement a non-verbal, natural means of expression. The desire to move to music should help to create in the withdrawn child a sense of uninhibited freedom and an inner harmony which he is sadly lacking.

As with any other handicapped child, the music should provoke in the disturbed one movements related to his experience, and lead to fantasy, to realistic imitations of specific movements, and to the expression of moods. A number of disturbed children are exhibitionists. We should allow them to display it, provided that they do not disturb the group. If one of them has some ability as a leader, the teacher should devise for him a prominent part entailing some responsibility towards the group.

Little by little music and movement should become an organized activity, planned for individual control and control of the group as in any musical activity. But in movement to music the child is left much more free to use his imagination and to choose his own interpretation of the music. Furthermore, moving together gives most children a sense of security and an instinctive pleasure.

At that stage the disturbed child has matured enough to become conscious of the harmony of movement he is able to achieve, and he may find in the emotional outlet the element of beauty and order that should accompany all musical experiences.

Dancing to music requires memory of steps related to musical patterns. The disturbed child whose intelligence is adequate can develop very much in this field if he is sensitive to music and can sustain his attention long enough to learn and to persevere. Then the emotional outlet is more satisfying because it carries a sense of purpose and achievement.

There are many forms of movement to music acceptable to the adolescent, not only those of a primitive kind, and we should not minimize their function in the life of the teenager. Ballet, mime to music, or impersonation through music and movement, are highly successful means of identification in which mind and emotions are at work together. This experience is on the border line of psychodrama, in which music sometimes plays a part but is not the motivating agent, and which therefore does not concern us here in spite of its great value to the handicapped child.

THE DEAF CHILD

The child who suffers from a sensory disability is very much handicapped with regard to movement to music. Music is to the deaf a series of vibrations perceived and transmitted to the brain through other channels than the auditory apparatus. Nevertheless these vibrations can carry a rhythm that corresponds to physical rhythm and may provoke in the deaf child rhythmical physical responses leading to pleasurable activities. Research in music and deafness has not been extensive because of the lack of workers who possess the necessary knowledge in the two fields. But some methods have been tried in several places. The training of the deaf child in the perception of rhythmical vibrations is done on much the same principles as with the normal child: namely through the organization into patterns of a series of sounds which take shape in time and can be remembered. The memory of these patterns developing in a certain order produces a feeling of anticipation, satisfaction, or surprise. This process is limited because the deaf child may not be able to apprehend more than the relative duration of the sounds. Nevertheless accentuation and volume, and perhaps a sense of pitch and of the overtones that produce tone colour may affect the deaf child in a way that we do not suspect.

Deafness produces deep frustration of all kinds throughout life. The perception of sound vibrations through other means than auditory may help the deaf child to communicate better with his environment, integrate, and lose his sense of loneliness.

THE BLIND CHILD

The blind child, unless he is retarded, often possesses the 'élan vital' which responds to the dynamics of music and movement. His disability has made him develop a great power of attention to sound and a memory of everything he hears. His sense of observation is focused on sound and physical contacts. He is therefore much aware of his body and learns how to move with care and skill.

The music teacher should be aware that the blind child has another conception of verbal expression than the normal child. Words to him do not suggest visual shapes or provoke mental images that are a help to children with sight. Words associated with music can add to the physical impulse of the blind child, but mostly in suggesting moods or ideas linked to a kinesthetic experience. The blind child can be said to be the only one to move to a purely musical experience.

A blind child aware of physical movement does not let himself go unconsciously and can achieve good motor control. If he knows that there is no physical obstacle in his way he can move to music with confidence and in freedom. He can also reproduce and memorize steps if they are quite clearly indicated in the music.

The education of the blind child aims at giving him as many contacts as possible with his environment, at creating in him a sense of space and distance through movements that are adaptable and responsive. He learns how to avoid accidents or bumping into people or things. A well-trained blind child is nimble and a pleasure to watch when he moves in his environment. Music can give purpose, meaning, and harmony to movements, through which he finds a natural way to express himself.

This cannot be achieved without much patient work. The removal of fear of movement is an essential part in the education of many handicapped children, of the cerebral palsied as much as the blind child. Because of its emotional appeal movement to music can give the blind child the desire to explore space through movement and to express himself without fear.

The blind child possesses many positive characteristics on which the music teacher can build music and movement; namely, his awareness of and sensibility to sound; his emotional and intellectual maturity; his memory of physical movement, and his motor control. Group work can be achieved with these children, who are usually sociable provided that they are familiar with the surroundings. The general principles are the same as with any other group except that a substitute must be found for visual experiences. The process of imitation or the use of imagination have to work in a sightless world.

Movement to music may be more to the blind child than an emotional outlet and an expression of life. It may also represent to him a conquest of space through an activity creating joy and harmony.

PERSONAL POSTSCRIPT

THE book is coming to an end, but this is not the end of the story. It will have failed if it does not produce better things for the maimed and deprived child.

I wanted to write this book because of the light I have seen in the eyes of handicapped children and the happiness I have watched grow on their faces during a musical experience. Music had created in them a joy that was deeper than fun and a happiness greater than enjoyment. I wish that more and more handicapped children could share in the gifts that music can give. This book is in essence a message from the children themselves, who have taught me all I know about them, and whose deprived life has been enriched by music. I speak on behalf of all who have gained something from music: of the little mongol girl who exclaimed at the end of a musical performance: 'This is smashing, I want more'; of the tormented child who found release in singing; of the spastics to whom the music lesson meant so much; of the little crippled dwarf who had passed Grade 4—and hundreds of others in need.

The sadness of a handicap is that it erects a wall which prevents us from fulfilling the needs of the child, needs that may be unconscious, hidden, unspoken, or painfully expressed. But music knows no barrier. It is an act of creation even to a little child whose body is crippled and whose mind is impaired. No child is too handicapped to be offered the gift that music can give him in so many ways.

But the gift must be presented in the manner appropriate to his condition, in order to be a true gift from which he will benefit in the present and the future. Love of the handicapped child is essential in those who care for him and want to help him through music. But more than love is needed. I have written this book with the deep conviction that the teacher or the therapist must possess psychological knowledge and musical skill if music for the handicapped child is to be a truly creative experience.

BIBLIOGRAPHY

BOOKS OR PAPERS ON MUSIC FOR HANDICAPPED CHILDREN

Alvin, Juliette, *Music Therapy* (Hutchinson, London 1975).

Bailey, Philip, *They Can Make Music* (Oxford University Press, London 1972).

Dobbs, J. P. B., *The Slow Learner and Music* (Oxford University Press, London 1966).

Dutoit, C. L. *Music, Movement, Therapy* (Dalcroze Society centenary edition, 1965).

Nordoff and Robbins, *Music Therapy in Special Education* (John Day Co., New York 1971).

Robins, F. and J., *Educational Rhythmics for Mentally Handicapped Children* (Édition Rappersville, Switzerland).

Ward, David, *Sound Approaches for Slow Learners* (Bedford Square Press Ltd., London 1972).

—— *Hearts and Hands and Voices: Music in the Education of Slow-Learning Children* (Oxford University Press, 1976).

—— *Singing in Special Schools* (Bedford Square Press Ltd., London 1973).

Publications of the British Society for Music Therapy, 48 Lanchester Road, London, N6 4TA.

  14 Sets of Conference papers from 1960.

  Project on Music with Severely Subnormal Boys (Juliette Alvin, 1970).

British Journal of Music Therapy.

Publications of National Association for Music Therapy (N.A.M.T.) U.S.A.

  Proceedings of yearly conferences 1952–1962 (Allen Press, P.O. Box 15, Lawrence, Kansas).

BOOKS ON MUSIC CONTAINING REFERENCES TO HANDICAPPED CHILDREN

Dalcroze, Jacques E., *La Musique et nous* (Perret Gentil, Geneva 1945).

Lundin, Robert W., *An Objective Psychology of Music* (Ronald Press Co. New York 1953).

Moore, Stephen, *Percussion Playing* (W. Paxton & Co., London 1959).

Willems, Edgar, *Les Bases psychologiques d'une éducation musicale* (Presses universitaires de France, 1956).

BOOKS ON HANDICAPPED CHILDREN
CONTAINING REFERENCES TO MUSIC

Bowley, Agatha H., *The Young Handicapped Child* (E. & S. Livingstone, Edinburgh 1957).

Burt, Sir Cyril, *The Backward Child* (University of London Press, London 1950).

Carson, Bernice Wells, and Gingeld, David R., *Play Activities for the Retarded Child* (Abingdon Press, Nashville, New York 1961).

Cleugh, Dr. M. G., *Teaching the Slow Learner* (Methuen & Co., London 1961).

Rassekh-Ardjomand, M. *L'Enfant problème* (Delachaux & Niestle, Geneva 1962).

Tansley, A. D., and Gulliford, R., *The Education of Slow Learning Children* (Routledge & Kegan Paul, 1960).

What is Special Education? Proceedings of 1966 International Conference (Association for Special Education).

Wing, J. K., *Early Childhood Autism* (Pergamon Press, 1966).

BOOKS OF GENERAL INTEREST

Bentley, Arnold, *Musical Ability in Children* (George Harrap & Co. 1966).

Furneaux, Barbara, *The Special Child* (Penguin, 1969).

Shaw-Lucas, W., *The Psychiatric Disorders of Childhood* (Butterworth, New York 1971).

Wall, W. J., *Education and Mental Health* (Unesco, 1960).

Wheeler, Dame Olive, *Mental Health and Education* (University of London Press, London 1961).